Managing like a Man

Women and Men in Corporate Management

JUDY WAJCMAN

Polity Press

First published in 1998 by Polity Press
in association with Blackwell Publishers Ltd.

Editorial office:
Polity Press
65 Bridge Street
Cambridge CB2 1UR, UK

Marketing and production:
Blackwell Publishers Ltd
108 Cowley Road
Oxford OX4 1JF, UK

ISBN 0-7456-1759-X
ISBN 0-7456-1760-3 (pbk)

A catalogue record for this book is available from the British Library.

Typeset in 10½ on 12 pt Times
by Best-set Typesetter Ltd., Hong Kong
Printed in Great Britain
by T.J. International, Padstow, Cornwall

This book is printed on acid-free paper.

Contents

Acknowledgements

I carried out the research for this book while I was a Principal Research Fellow at the Industrial Relations Research Unit (IRRU), University of Warwick, which is a research centre of the Economic and Social Research Council. This was an excellent workplace for me, providing a stimulating and scholarly community in which to undertake research on employment. All members of the unit made me welcome. I would particularly like to thank Paul Edwards, Linda Dickens, Sonia Liff, Paul Marginson, Helen Newell, Keith Sisson, Jeremy Waddington and Colin Whitston.

I would never have chosen to study managers if not for the encouragement of Paul Edwards. He took a keen interest throughout the project and carefully read the various drafts through which this book has metamorphosed. I thank him especially for making my time at IRRU so productive. Val Jephcott contributed invaluable assistance in the preparation of the data analysis, while Lesley Williams gave outstanding administrative support. Sonia Liff sharpened my thinking on equal employment opportunities and Helen Newell navigated me through the murky waters of management discourse. For the duration of my fellowship I enjoyed extended hospitality in Coventry from Paul Marginson, who shared my penchant for discussing political economy over breakfast. It is exactly what every woman needs to start the day!

The companies who participated in the survey and the managers who talked to me must remain anonymous, but I wish to acknowledge their cooperation and interest. In particular, I am indebted to the managers I interviewed for this study, who were generous with their time and helpful with accounts of their experiences.

The ideas in chapter 1 were developed with Sonia Liff and our discussion of some of the themes is published as Liff and Wajcman, ' "Sameness" and "difference" revisited: which way forward for equal opportunity initiatives?', *Journal of Management Studies*, 33/1 (1996), pp. 79–94. Earlier versions of parts of this book have appeared as 'Women and men managers: careers and equal opportunities', in R. Crompton, D. Gallie and K. Purcell (eds), *Changing Forms of Employment* (London: Routledge, 1996), pp. 259–77; 'Desperately seeking differences: is management style gendered?', *British Journal of Industrial Relations*, 34/3 (1996), pp. 333–49; 'The domestic basis for the managerial career', *Sociological Review*, 44. 4 (1996), pp. 609–29. While at Warwick I organized a workshop, the papers from which appear as 'Organisations, gender and power', Warwick Papers in Industrial Relations, no. 48, Dec. 1993. I thank the participants. I am also grateful to the many feminist colleagues and friends around the world who have collectively enriched the sociology of work and employment by subjecting it to a gender analysis.

Much of the book was written after I returned to Australia, having been appointed to a Chair in Sociology at the Research School of Social Sciences at the Australian National University. I very much appreciate the resources that this has provided me with, alas available to too few women. I owe special thanks to Lisa Adkins and Carol Johnson, who commented on various drafts and patiently engaged with ideas in the book, adding to it significantly. Frank Jones also read the manuscript and did a scrupulous editing job. Katerina Agostino and Digby Duncan provided excellent and enthusiastic research assistance.

Jenny Earle once more lived through the writing of a book, reading, discussing and tirelessly editing as we moved between London, Coventry, Zurich and Canberra. I thank her for managing!

Introduction

The feminization of the paid labour force has been heralded as one of the most important social changes in the twentieth century. Many argue that women's new-found economic independence is revolutionary. It has been accompanied by a profound cultural shift, with the emergence of a new consciousness and widespread public discourse about gender equity. A liberal commitment to equality between the sexes is now broadly accepted and is even enshrined in law.

Western societies have achieved some progress towards gender equity in the public sphere of the labour market. In the private sphere, intimate relations are changing as well, with modern marriages said to be taking a new companionate form. What it means to be a man or a woman is no longer ordained by 'nature'. Gendered identities have undergone a major transformation.

Even so, as we approach the end of the twentieth century, men continue to monopolize the elite levels of corporate power in almost all regions of the world. While the legitimacy of patriarchy has been eroded, it is far from being rendered obsolete. The material and institutional structures of patriarchy are still largely intact.

How can we even begin to understand the persistence of sexual inequality within an explicit framework of equality? This book suggests that an investigation of the gender relations of senior management in a 'post-feminist' age can be instructive for a number of reasons. Firstly, the managerial job is a repository of power and authority, the site of decision-making and rule-making within organizations. Women's access to senior management is both a symbol and a measure of organizational change. Over recent decades women have entered lower and middle managerial levels in large numbers without major disruption to the ways organizations operate. Only when they are present at the top are they perceived as a direct threat and challenge to male power. After being excluded for so long, women who have gained institutional power may make a difference to the way the job is done. How differently do men respond to women sharing what remains largely male territory?

Secondly, to study senior women managers is to study exceptional women in an atypical context. They inhabit a corporate world that is very male dominated, and they are inevitably disruptive to the status quo. When a woman occupies a position traditionally filled by a man, the significance of her sex, for both how she operates and how she is treated, is subjected to scrutiny in a way that the 'normal' hierarchical order is not. The usually hidden processes and tensions of gender relations at work are likely to be more visible in high-technology multinationals where women are breaking new ground.

Finally, there is an increasing preoccupation in both feminist theory and organization theory with questions of culture and subjectivity. These issues are particularly critical to management, because managers are deemed to have certain attributes and personalities, and a certain leadership style. After all, what managers do most of the time is communicate directly with people. So sharing a common language and understanding is crucial. Management literature is now preoccupied with the dynamics of cultural change within organizations and how to harness it in the pursuit of profit.

This book is innovatory in several respects. A key argument of the book is that management incorporates a male standard that positions women as out of place. Indeed, the construction of women as different from men is one of the mechanisms whereby male power in the workplace is maintained. There is now an extensive literature on women and management, much of it prescriptive in nature. However, most of this writing is exclusively about women managers, treated in isolation from men. Quarantining women in this way has the effect of locating women as the problem, and reinforces assumptions that men are uniformly to the management-manner born. This book is unique in comparing men and women in similar senior managerial positions. It is a study of men and women who work alongside each other doing the same jobs, encompassing the experiences of both sexes in the managerial hierarchy. Since masculinity and femininity are inherently relational concepts, with meaning only in relation to each other, this study is then able to analyse the gender regimes of management.

I use the concept gender regime (a term introduced by Connell 1987) as a shorthand for institutionalized power relations between men and women where gender is a property of institutions and historical processes, as well as of individuals. Gendering processes are involved in how jobs and careers are constituted, both in the symbolic order and in organizational practices (discursive and material), and these power relations are embedded in the subjective gender identity of managers.

The nexus between work and home in the formation of particular gender regimes is central to the argument. Although studies of the workplace and research on family and home life are now well developed, these areas have become separate specialisms within sociology. This book examines the interconnections between home and employment within a single framework and presents substantial material on the home lives of managers. In addition, I bring together insights developed on gender and work from perspectives in different disciplines. Thus I draw on industrial relations, on organizational behaviour and management studies, as well as on sociological and feminist analyses.

The research is based on a study of managers in high-technology multinational companies that boast sophisticated equal opportunity policies and are formally committed to their implementation. However, this project is not simply an evaluation of sex equality strategies in the workplace. Rather, it is a comparative analysis of men's and women's experience in a changing corporate climate.

I approached five major companies, all of which agreed to participate. Although located in Britain, they are global companies with strikingly similar approaches to the management of labour. The companies are all multinationals, and indeed the firm where most of the data were collected, the case study company, is US owned. Although multinationals' behaviour in relation to labour is shaped by the regulatory systems of particular nation-states, there seems to be a general move away from hierarchical organization towards a more flexible structure. Corporate restructuring, accompanied by organizational 'delayering' and the decline of the long-term, single-organization career, is the common trend in capitalist economies. The organizational processes which are reshaping management in the UK mirror those operating in American, European or Australian firms. The central issues raised in the book, therefore, are not specific to one country but have a much wider relevance.

The companies operate in the technologically advanced sectors of oil, chemicals and computing services, and were selected for the following reasons. Firstly, they are companies widely acknowledged to be at the forefront of equal opportunity policies. So the project set out to study best practice companies. Secondly, it seemed appropriate and timely to examine the private sector. Most existing research in this area deals with the public sector, for example, the British National Health Service. Finally, it is often claimed that the new fast-growing high-tech industries provide easier access to women managers than those that have inherited long-standing organizational structures.

This research adopts a questionnaire survey methodology. However, I also draw extensively on qualitative data derived from in-depth interviews conducted during 1994 with 20 women and men managers in the case study company. The interviewees, who participated in the survey, exhibit characteristics typical of the profile of the overall sample. A full description of the case study company, which I have called 'Chip', can be found in chapter 4.

The use of the term 'manager' varies considerably from one organizational setting to another. In some it is used to designate levels of status or personal prestige, while in others it delineates a variety of functional responsibilities (see, for example, Nicholson and West 1988; Stewart 1967). Generally the term describes those who, in one way or another, and to varying degrees, coordinate and control the behaviour of others. For this study I accepted the definition used by the organizations themselves. Senior managers, the subject of this study, are those earning over £40,000 a year in 1993. This level of managerial salary is consistent across the five companies involved, all of which recognized £40,000 as the cut-off between senior and middle management. Given how few women there are in the most senior positions, this definition also allowed for a reasonable sample size. It produced a remarkably similar number of women (on average 24) across all the companies. Although the companies in the study would be regarded as 'leading edge' cases, in fact women are still seriously underrepresented at senior levels of management in all those selected for analysis.

The questionnaires were sent to 439 managers between October and December 1993.[1] All of the senior women managers and a representative sample of men in equivalent grades were surveyed. A total of 324 managers completed the questionnaire: 108 women and 216 men. The response rate of 74 per cent (89% for the women and 68% for the men) is exceptional for a mailback questionnaire, indicating a high level of interest in the subject matter of the survey. Male managers were included, both in their own right and as a control group in relation to the women. A simple random sample of the men would have been, on average, more senior than their female counterparts. So a crucial element in the research design was matching the sample of men so that they were similar to the women in all respects other than gender. The findings presented here are based on the aggregate data from the five companies, and all the differences referred to in this paper reach the conventional (5%) level of statistical significance. They are unlikely to be due to chance.

The profile of women who have achieved senior management positions in all the companies is broadly similar to that of their male colleagues. Crucially, as stated above, the research design controls for differences in managerial level. In terms of age, the highest proportion of managers in the survey (56%) is in the 35–44 age group (see table I.1), reflecting the age distribution for this occupational group in national labour force surveys. Women managers tend to be younger and have joined the organization more recently. However, there is no sex difference in the age of first managerial appointment: 87 per cent of both men and women reach managerial level by the age of 35. Respondents move around within the company. Over 80 per cent of both men and women were recruited to their present post through internal promotion. Indeed, over 60 per cent of the sample have been with their company more than a decade. So men and women have had equal exposure to the promotion system in their company.

While human capital theory emphasizes women's supposed lack of qualifications, recent studies have found that women are generally better qualified in formal terms for equivalent jobs. However, no gender differences in educational qualifications emerge in this study, with almost half the respondents having degrees and a further third having some sort of postgraduate qualification. With regard to the related issue of training, once again the same proportion (74%) of

Table I.1 Percentage distribution of respondents according to their age

Age categories	Men	Women
Under 25	0	0
25–34	9	23
35–44	56	56
45–54	33	21
55 and over	2	0

I.2 Percentage distribution of respondents in terms of principal management function

Functional specialism	Men	Women
Administration/company secretary	1	2
Management services	1	0
Finance/accounting	9	12
Education/training	1	2
Personnel/HR/IR	5	14
Production/manufacturing	2	2
Computing/IT	10	7
Development/strategic affairs	8	7
Marketing/sales	31	21
Corporate affairs/public relations	2	4
Management consultancy	4	6
General management	24	18
Other	2	5

both men and women have taken a training course that they themselves had suggested for their own self-development, financed by the company.

Respondents were asked about their job title. A higher proportion of men than women describe themselves as managers (85% of men and 69% of women), whereas 31 per cent of the women describe themselves as functional specialists. A substantial proportion of both men and women in the study describe themselves as 'general managers' (26% and 20% respectively). When asked about their principal management function (see table I.2) the women are more likely to report being in personnel/human resources and service functions, whereas men are more likely to report being in marketing and sales. These responses broadly reflect the wider labour market patterns of gender specialization in management function, although if anything there is a smaller concentration of women in the human resources function than one might expect (see Legge 1987).

However, there is a marked sex difference in the numbers of people for whom the respondents are directly responsible. Whereas 64 per cent of the women manage fewer than 10 people, this is true for under half of the men. Over 20 per cent of the men manage more than 50 employees, whereas only 12 per cent of the women carry similar managerial responsibilities. Men are more than twice as likely as women to have responsibility for over 100 employees. So even at the same managerial level, men are given greater managerial responsibilities than women. It should be noted, however, that this is not independent of management function. As more of the women are professional specialists, they are less likely to have extensive responsibilities for subordinate employees.

The research findings from this project specifically inform the arguments developed in chapters 3 to 6. While the original empirical research presented here is fundamental to the argument I am making, it is not possible to address all the relevant issues that bear upon the topic through a single set of data. So I have situated my data within the wider context of contemporary theoretical debates in this area, as well as drawing upon and bringing together the broad range of other recent findings on managers in large firms.

The book begins with an overview of the theory and practice of sex equality in organizations. In this first chapter, I review feminist debates about whether we should aspire to equality based on sameness as, or difference from, men and the political consequences of adopting one or other of these positions. I argue that these academic theories cannot simply be translated into a feminist practice on equal opportunities. Rather, we should reject the sameness/difference dichotomy and focus instead on policies that challenge the norms of male work patterns. Even the recent focus of equality initiatives, managing diversity, still holds men up as the standard against which women are measured and found wanting. This standard has to be radically challenged. In the following chapters, I explore how gender is threaded through the fabric of organizations and the managerial job, and suggest ways in which this pattern might be changed.

Chapter 2 assesses conventional explanations of women's underrepresentation, or men's overrepresentation, in the higher levels of management. I go beyond the orthodox analysis that invokes the unequal domestic division of labour, to argue that the 'sexual contract' constitutes women and men as fundamentally different kinds of workers. I then discuss recent developments in organization theory that focus on the construction of masculinity and femininity at work. Management is an occupation historically and culturally associated with men. It is seen as intrinsically masculine, something only men (can) do. The very language of management is resolutely masculine. Organizations are then a crucial site for the ordering of gender, and for the establishment and preservation of male power.

In this book I have also used the term management to describe the organization of domestic work in the household. I do this for two reasons. One is to highlight the sex-biased definition of management which, like the established usage of 'work', refers to paid employment in the labour market. The other reason is that it also draws attention to the increasing commodification of domestic tasks within the home.

The question of whether women are becoming more like men or are 'doing it differently' has been popularized in discussions about whether high-flying women bring a distinctive female style of management to organizations. Chapter 3 examines the thesis that management style is itself gendered, in terms of whether there are differences in how women and men actually manage. After placing these arguments in the wider context of corporate restructuring in the 1990s, I conclude that the similarities between women and men who have achieved senior management positions far outweigh any differences between women and men as groups. This commonality comes about because women's presence in the world of men is conditional on them being willing to modify their behaviour to become more like men. If there are no significant sex differences in management style, in what ways are women disadvantaged by the fact that they are not men?

Chapter 4 takes issue with the argument that men and women have a profoundly different orientation to paid employment, and that work is more central to men's identity. The women and men in my study have similar career patterns and are equally highly motivated. What needs explaining is why, in general, women's experience of organizational life is so different from that of their male colleagues. The systematic difference here is that women encounter sex-specific obstacles to promotion opportunities. Although men's attitudes towards formal equality for women managers are by and large favourable, there is a divergence between such attitudes and organizational reality. I explore how the masculinist assumptions underlying management structures and practices continue to marginalize and exclude women from senior management roles.

Organizations are infused with sexuality and emotion. Chapter 5 considers how relationships between the sexes are negotiated, including the way sexual harassment is dealt with in an equal opportunity environment. The motif of women's 'difference' is explored further here. I argue that women are sexualized in a way that men are not, and that male sexual imagery pervades the symbolic order of organizations. As a result, women managers face the contradictory demands of being feminine and being businesslike. Their authority is always in question and under threat. In male-dominated companies such as those in my study, this problem is particularly acute.

Echoing themes from the previous three chapters, chapter 6 presents an analysis of the management of home life. An emphasis on the gendering of jobs and the masculinity of organizations should not distract us from the extent to which opportunities in the labour market are shaped by people's family commitments and aspirations. In this chapter, I examine the extensive and complex domestic arrangements necessary to sustain the life of a senior manager and find that the occupation itself is premised on a particular organization of family life. The pressures of combining work and home responsibilities affect men as well as women. However, men and women do not have the same relationship to the domestic sphere and this domestic inequality has far-reaching consequences for their ability to be equal at work. The differences between men and women managers are much more marked in how they manage their household than in how they manage at work.

In the conclusion, I reflect on the contradictory nature of women's relationship to power. On the one hand, management as an occupation has been opened up to women, providing fresh possibilities. On the other hand, power and authority, while taking new forms, remain gendered as male. While sex equality policies in the workplace have not been transformative in themselves, they have been crucial in contesting and making more transparent the established gender order in organizations.

Note

1   All the managers in the sample are 'white'. This book is about the gender relations of management. Many of the issues I raise could be related to the ethnic and racial characteristics of senior managers. Hence the absence of non-white managers in the sample reflects reality at the level of management studied here.

1

Sex Equality in Organizations

One of the central tenets of the contemporary women's movement is that sexual inequality is tied to the fact that in every society men and women largely do different kinds of work. Indeed, sex segregation in the labour market is now a subject of mainstream quantitative sociology. Existing divisions have tended to result in studies of work and employment that look at men and women in isolation from each other. This research looks at women and men doing the same work and is thus an excellent basis for evaluating the impact of equal opportunity policies, and comparing the experiences of the sexes and their relationship to the organization.

The entry of women into senior management has generated much popular debate about whether they are 'making a difference' to the way organizations are run. The emphasis has shifted from encouraging women to emulate a male leadership style to asserting the value of qualities characterized as feminine that women bring to management. This bipolar framework of sameness or difference can be seen in other responses to the barriers women face at work. Different family commitments are traditionally the reason cited for women not reaching senior levels. Some argue that with the advent of 'family friendly' policies, women can now have the same careers as men. Others argue that a separate 'mommy track' should be provided to accommodate the different careers of women. This stance fits well with the emergent policy of fostering diverse and pluralistic patterns of work and careers that are equally valued. In the present chapter I explore the extent to which the theory and practice of equal opportunities, as currently conceived, address these questions and problems. Reflections on feminist thinking about sameness and difference, equality and diversity, are important here and as a thread woven throughout the text.

It may be taken as an indication of the success of equal opportunity legislation and policies that this study is possible. There are now some women at the top. Yet a marked gender imbalance persists at the apex of organizational career structures. Conventional equality initiatives have had a limited impact on women's position in the workforce. There is not much room at the top for women, and we shall see that successful women are not so much representatives of, as exiles from, their sex.

The drive for 'equal opportunities' within organizations has been decried as too limited a strategy in some quarters, while provoking strong opposition in others. Its central objective is to break down the sexual division of labour and this makes it a controversial reform. It involves dismantling the barriers that block horizontal movement by women into male-dominated areas of work, as well as those that prevent their vertical progress to higher levels in organizational hierarchies. Its implementation means opening up access to the organization by fair recruitment practices, providing training courses for women, and reviewing appraisal and promotion procedures. Such initiatives should result in an increase in the numbers of women in senior professional and managerial positions, and greater recognition of their competence and authority.

It is now widely acknowledged that these policies have not achieved the changes they are supposed to achieve. In this chapter I discuss the theoretical frameworks within which equal opportunity policy has developed. Feminists have long debated whether women's subordination can best be overcome by a focus on equality as sameness with men, or by a recognition of sex difference. We will see that arguments based on sameness and on difference have always been in play, and are apt to be invoked according to their strategic utility in particular circumstances. Both approaches, however, position women as the problem and accept men's life experience as the norm. They fail to challenge the conceptualization of work, and of organizations, as gender neutral. The title of this book, *Managing like a Man*, proclaims the profoundly gendered character of an apparently neutral occupation from which women have been largely excluded, namely, managerial work.

From Equal Opportunities to Positive Discrimination

Legislation against sex discrimination in the United Kingdom dates from the 1970s. The Equal Pay Act 1970, which came into effect in

1975, made it unlawful to discriminate between women and men in pay or other terms of their contracts of employment. It specified that women were entitled to the same pay as men if doing the same or broadly similar work. A companion Act, the Sex Discrimination Act 1975, made it unlawful to treat women less favourably than men (or married people less favourably than single people) in education, training or employment, or in the provision of goods, facilities or services. It introduced a concept of indirect discrimination, which is deemed to occur when an employer applies to both sexes a condition of a kind such that the proportion of one sex who can comply with it is considerably smaller. In 1976 the Race Relations Act was passed, introducing the same provisions in relation to ethnic minorities as those applying to women.

This legislation and other influences such as labour market changes have stimulated the development of equal opportunity policies at the organizational level. These policies emerged as a response to shortcomings in anti-discrimination legislation, such as the reactive nature of anti-discrimination laws and the reliance on individual complaint. The provision of equal opportunities, by contrast, is described as proactive intervention to create a non-discriminatory environment.

In the UK formal policies are usually initiated and controlled by personnel/human resource departments and tend to follow a common format based on the codes of practice issued by the Equal Opportunities Commission and the Commission for Racial Equality. These policies outline procedural approaches to avoid discrimination and promote equality. The first part is based on the steps considered necessary to comply with the anti-discrimination legislation. The second part outlines those initiatives compatible with, but not required by, the legislation which are thought likely to enhance the opportunities of previously disadvantaged groups. Such policies are now widespread and form part of normal business practice, particularly among large organizations. A recent company-level industrial relations survey found that 75 per cent of those surveyed had an equal opportunity policy in place (Marginson et al. 1993).

Signs of progress towards greater equality of opportunity in employment can also be seen in the growth of Opportunity 2000. This business-led campaign was launched in 1991 with support from the Conservative government, to 'increase the quality and quantity of women's participation in the workforce' by the year 2000. Its focus has been on higher management. The organization claims to include the most progressive UK companies and counts among its founder members a quarter of *The Times* Top One Hundred Companies. As for the companies, membership enhances their profile and encourages the efficient use of human resources. By 1997, over 300 organizations from both the public and private sectors were members. Together they employed over a quarter of the UK workforce (Business in the Community 1996). Almost one-third of these member companies now offer flexible work arrangements; half provide some kind of childcare or career break option; and almost all provide some form of training or education designed to increase women's opportunities at work.

The dominant approach to gender equality at work is most commonly characterized as 'equal treatment'. Enshrined within the liberal legal tradition, anti-discrimination legislation provides the right, on an individual basis, to be treated the same as a person of the opposite sex in the same circumstances. The way that anti-discrimination legislation has interpreted treating 'like as like' is that people should be judged not by their gender or ethnicity but by their job-related capacities. In practice this has led 'liberal' policies to focus on the development of techniques to ensure that women are assessed in the same way as men. Jewson and Mason (1986) extend this analysis to equal opportunities initiatives more broadly, calling the dominant policy approach 'liberal'. This model, common to North America and Western Europe, regards current inequalities as distortions of the rational, efficient workings of the market, which can be corrected by increasing bureaucratic controls: formalizing and standardizing recruitment, promotion and training procedures.

Many feminists have pointed out that equal opportunities policies take an oversimplistic view both of the problem of inequality (seeing it as a managerial failure to treat like as like) and its solution ('equality' can be achieved by treating women the same as men). They have designated the legislation and associated policies as offering only 'formal equality'.

Feminism in the 1970s was characterized by a profound ambivalence towards the notion of 'equality', and the value of liberal-democratic reform. While the movement formulated demands for an end to discrimination, legal rights and financial independence for women, and while it actively promoted equality legislation, there was scepticism about both the possibility and the desirability of equality with men. In my view the goal was neither feasible nor desirable. Sameness is judged against a unitary standard of male characteristics and behaviour. As Pateman (1988: 231) expressed it: 'women's equal standing must be accepted as an expression of the freedom of women *as women*, and not treated as an indication that women can be just like men.'

These issues have been further complicated by the fact that feminist theorists have become increasingly concerned that the category 'women', which is invoked in equal opportunity policies, falsely universalizes women's experience (Eisenstein 1984; Nicholson 1990; Riley 1988; Young 1990). After all, policies based on sameness/equal treatment require women to deny, or attempt to minimize, differences between themselves and men as the price of equality. Avoiding the accusation of essentialism, or the assertion of fixed, unified and opposed female and male natures, seems to be at the heart of much contemporary feminist theory and politics. In the words of Schor (1994: xiii), 'can there be a feminist politics that dispenses with the notion of Woman?' Indeed, according to Bacchi (1996), there is now an almost insurmountable rift between feminist policy-makers and feminist theorists, with the former campaigning for 'women' and the latter disputing the legitimacy of the same project.

This critique of equality based on sameness provides important insights into the limitations of many equal opportunity initiatives. It is, however, a position that is difficult to sustain across the range of activities being pursued under the label of equal opportunities (Liff and Wajcman 1996). Even the anti-discrimination law, which seems to be straightforwardly about treating women the same as men would be treated in the same circumstances, arguably goes further and acknowledges women's difference in some circumstances.

The equal value amendment to the UK Equal Pay Act is a case in point. The original legislation provided for equal pay on an equal treatment basis, that is, the same pay for doing the same job. Since occupational segregation means that women are rarely in the same situation as men, the original legislation had little effect on pay differentials. The equal value amendment rules that people in different jobs involving comparable skill, responsibility, working conditions and effort should receive equal benefits in terms of pay. Since jobs can be judged to be of equal value while being different in terms of other characteristics like type of work or qualifications required, it is difficult to treat this situation as a case of equal pay being awarded to people in the same situation.

Similar tensions arise from trying to fit the range of equality initiatives seen in many organizations within the 'equal treatment'/'sameness' definition. In practice many go beyond formalizing selection and other personnel procedures to ensure equal treatment for women who, in all aspects apart from their gender, are the same as men in terms of their suitability for a post. Organizations which are proactive on equality issues have stretched and reinterpreted the equal treatment model in a number of ways.

One set of initiatives could be said to be aimed at reducing the barriers which prevent men and women from achieving the same goal. Here we could include the provision of childcare and other measures to reduce the difficulty of combining waged work with domestic commitments. Also in this category one could include single-sex training schemes to provide women with the skills required to gain entry to occupations in which they have traditionally been seriously underrepresented. Many people object to such schemes, arguing that if women have to be 'helped' to be like men, then such initiatives constitute not equal treatment but an unfair advantage. Even so, all these things can lawfully be provided (although, of course, they are not required).

In other cases organizations are examining job requirements and conditions in more radical ways than those required by indirect dis-crimination clauses, in an attempt to ensure that women are able to fulfil the requirements. Such initiatives include the removal of certain formal qualifications, such as a degree, unless it can be proved that the job could not be done by someone with a different set of experi-ences. Jobs which were traditionally worked on a full-time basis have been opened up to those wishing to work part-time or job share. The argument here is that it is very difficult for women to gain equal treatment because job conditions are constructed around men's skills and patterns of work (Webb and Liff 1988). These changes aim to make requirements more 'neutral' so that women are more likely to be in the same situation (able to satisfy job requirements) and thus qualify for equal treatment (access to jobs).

If feminists are critical of these initiatives, studies report that men experience them not as equal treatment but as a lowering of stand-ards, or rewriting the rules to suit women. Men commonly express the view that equal opportunity has 'gone too far' and that women are being appointed in preference to men. It is perhaps obvious that groups who currently have a dominant position in the workforce are likely to feel threatened by equal opportunity initiatives. Those who have been successful in gaining jobs and progressing up organiza-tional hierarchies generally feel that they have achieved their posi-tions as a result of their own merits. They may be quite happy for other individuals to do the same regardless of their gender or ethni-city but are concerned about policies which they see as giving these groups special help.

Men's resistance to sex equality is thoroughly explored in Cockburn's (1991) study of change in four organizations. She found widespread annoyance with maternity leave and related provisions such as special leave, part-time work and job sharing. Many male managers felt maternity leave and flexibility were now 'too generous' and were 'fed up to the back teeth' with the continual absences of women for 'one thing or another'. 'There is a deep-rooted feeling among many men at all levels that pregnant women and new mothers are "cheating", "taking us for a ride" or generally "messing the organisation around". Yet sick leave, which is more frequent and less predictable than maternity leave does not incur the same blame' (Cockburn 1991: 94). Recent surveys carried out in universities in Australia and the Netherlands found that many academic men believe that women are unfairly advantaged by current equal opportunity hiring practices (Bacchi 1996: 28). It would seem that even modest policies that attempt to place women and men on the same footing can provoke a backlash.

Current anti-discrimination legislation and equal opportunity initiatives draw primarily on an equal treatment/sameness notion of equality. There are of course, as these examples show, important elements within them which demonstrate an awareness of the limitations of such a naive perspective. It is evident that sex equality policies are more complex than the sameness/difference arguments would allow. However, a conception of equal opportunity which requires individuals to be treated the same can never adequately address the fact that women are situated differently. Ignoring women's relationship to the private sphere, for example, conceals the way women are penalized for their difference. Unless difference is recognized and taken account of, women will not be able to compete equally. As they stand, equal opportunity policies can only mean assimilation to a pre-existing and problematic male norm. Indeed, a more radical approach is taken in a number of countries where the emphasis is on confronting difference and where special treatment or positive discrimination is mandatory.

'Hard' Affirmative Action

Leading equality policies in the United States, Canada, Australia, Sweden, the Netherlands and Norway are analysed by Bacchi (1996) in her recent book *The Politics of Affirmative Action*. The term 'affirmative action' originated in the United States, but because of the increasing opposition it provoked, many countries have sought to distance themselves from the term. Other terminology has been adopted such as employment equity, equal opportunities and now positive action, as it is commonly described throughout Europe. In all the countries Bacchi studied, the stated goal of labour market affirmative action programmes is to encourage women into non-traditional jobs, that is, jobs traditionally performed by men, and to increase their access to positions of higher pay and status. There are generally said to be two kinds of affirmative action programmes, 'soft' programmes and 'hard' or 'strong' programmes. The former refers to programmes which increase the possibility that members of underrepresented groups will be appointed or promoted. These include initiatives such as recruitment policies or training programmes to assist disadvantaged groups to compete more effectively. Hard programmes are those specifying that being a member of an underrepresented group *counts* in assessing candidates for appointments and promotions. Quotas are one form of preferential hiring and promotion. This type of policy explicitly recognizes that equality can be understood as treating (different) people as different.

Federal contractors in the USA were first required to devise and carry out affirmative action programmes in the late 1960s. Executive Order 11246, signed into law in 1965 by President Johnson, barred discrimination on the basis of race, colour, religion, or national origin in federal employment contractors and subcontractors. The order requires executive departments and agencies to 'maintain a *positive* program of equal opportunities'. In 1967 the Order was expanded to include sex discrimination. This was strengthened by the Equal Opportunity Act of 1972 which empowered the Civil Service Commission to review and approve equal opportunity plans and to monitor the progress of federal agencies and departments in achieving equal opportunities for women and minorities.

Affirmative action is a process which involves at least three steps. The first is to analyse an employer's workforce to determine whether the percentages of sex, race, or ethnic groups in specific job classifications correspond to the percentages of those groups generally prevailing in the relevant labour market. Second, if some of the groups are manifestly underrepresented, the employer's entire personnel process is scrutinized to identify the particular procedures responsible for the disproportionate figures. Third, if the employer finds that elements of the personnel process tend to exclude a group, a broad range of race- or gender-conscious measures may be undertaken to remedy the imbalance. These include adoption of goals and timetables for recruitment, training, hiring and promotion of minorities and women, a recruitment programme to attract members of the excluded groups, and an effective monitoring system.

Feminists have argued for positive discrimination/affirmative action as a legitimate remedy to overcome the effects of past discrimination and the only way to achieve 'genuine' as opposed to mere 'formal' equality. This approach requires programmes aimed at enhancing the competitive chances of the members of socially disadvantaged groups in access to education and in the processes of recruitment, selection and promotion in employment. Its purpose is to break the cycle created by the tendency of those in power to appoint and promote people like themselves. While the policies adopted, particularly in the US, have been impressive, they have had limited impact on sex segregation in senior management.

It is important to understand the origins of positive discrimination in the US as a response primarily to the historic subordination and enslavement of black people. Strong measures were seen as legitimate to remedy the effects of gross discrimination in the past. In this context, 'women' are regarded as another 'minority' group against whom discrimination will not be permitted, rather than as a starting point for policy formulation in this area. This understanding is reflected both in the theoretical literature on affirmative action, and in its practice, both of which mainly focus on race issues. This construction of affirmative action opens the door to invidious comparisons as to the relative disadvantage of women and other 'minority' groups. It may further divide the already fragmented powerless groups. 'Setting "women" against other outgroups minimizes change in at least two ways. First, the "spoils" are to be divvied up. And second, only those who can manage to fit their case to established categories of "disadvantage" get heard' (Bacchi 1996: 49).

Furthermore, the predominant understanding is that affirmative action means 'preferential treatment' to assist 'disadvantaged' people to move into better jobs. In this discourse of affirmative action, the 'beneficiaries' become the problem. As Radin (1991: 134) says: 'the dominant ordinary language view is that affirmative action gives benefits to people who are less qualified or less deserving than white men or indeed are wholly unqualified or undeserving.' Such an approach assumes that appointment procedures as currently implemented are objective and form an exclusive basis for the assessment of individual suitability. In practice, this is usually understood to mean that the merit principle forms the basis for appointment to positions and for promotions. This understanding of affirmative action as assistance to the 'needy' also accepts a broad vision of society as open to opportunities, except in a few instances.

Contrary to this view, a concern of this book is to challenge the apparent neutrality of selection procedures and criteria. Many years of feminist theorizing have established that definitions of merit and skill are not fixed but depend on the power of particular groups who define them (Cockburn 1985; Phillips and Taylor 1980; Young 1990). The specification of job requirements requires subjective judgements about necessary skills and working practices: decisions which may result in the job becoming gendered. 'Merit' is rarely defined. Indeed, one might say it is the 'black box' of the equal opportunities process, the key to its functioning (Burton 1991). Outgroups remain outgroups because ingroups assess them by reference to their own image. Studies have shown that selectors continue to hold stereotypes of women and men which affect their decision-making, and have difficulty conceptualizing job requirements in gender-neutral terms (Collinson et al. 1990; Curran 1988).

In subsequent chapters I will look in more detail at how jobs themselves, and the qualities which are sought in applicants, are sex-typed. Suffice it to say here that notions of suitability are socially constructed and inseparable from the acceptability of candidates (Webb and Liff 1988).Viewed thus, affirmative action is not 'preferential' treatment but an acknowledgement that power and bias are at work in appointments.

However, despite being a more proactive strategy, affirmative action remains subject to limitations similar to those afflicting conventional equal opportunity reforms. Even at its 'hardest', affirmative action still involves moving members of disadvantaged groups up the ladder while leaving the structure of the ladder unchanged. It stops short of questioning the processes by which institutional power is claimed and distributed.

Currently affirmative action faces increasing opposition and is fast losing ground in the US. Critics portray it as inappropriate and excessively interventionist, going against the grain of the American equal opportunities myth. The conservative attack is shifting popular opinion against hard affirmative action. Only 'soft' measures, which seek to alleviate sex discrimination through advocating gender-neutral or 'same' treatment, are now legitimate. Compensating individuals for past social and educational disadvantages rooted in difference now seems contrary to the principle of merit. Disenchantment with affirmative action in the workplace in the US has led to the recent interest in 'managing diversity'. It is to this new model of equal opportunities that we now turn.

Managing Diversity

If affirmative action was the policy of the 1980s, 'diversity management' is replacing it as the policy of the 1990s. In North America, and increasingly in Britain and Australia, the intention of equality initiatives is to value or manage 'diversity', which purports to be a positive valuing of differences between people. In a key article in *Harvard Business Review*, Thomas describes the new way forward 'From affirmative action to affirming diversity': 'The goal is to manage diversity in such as way as to get from a diverse work force the same productivity we once got from a homogeneous work force, and do it without artificial programs, standards – or barriers' (1990: 112).

Proponents of this approach argue that businesses are limiting themselves by continuing to employ only people in the same mould as those already in place. Women and ethnic minorities, it is argued, can bring new strengths to a workforce and help organizations maintain their competitive edge. Rather than being rejected, difference should be managed effectively.

Compared with over 20 years of 'equal opportunities' initiatives, 'managing diversity' strategies are still in their infancy and it is not always easy to distinguish reality from rhetoric. In an early contribution to the US debate, Copeland (1988b) describes ten measures typically included in a 'valuing diversity' programme. Most of these would not be out of place in any broadly based equal opportunity policy. They focus on initiatives to recruit people from under-represented groups, activities in the community to develop a good public image with these groups, providing 'high flying' women and minorities with access to career development track jobs, mentoring, executive appointments to get underrepresented groups through the 'glass ceiling', training for managers to counter stereotypes and increase their understanding of organizational barriers, and ensuring that organizational provisions such as holidays and food are inclusive of the needs of all. In the case of the others, the language may be different but the underlying concept is not. For example, diversity training for employees is said to 'improve employees' understanding of corporate culture, success requirements, and career choices that will affect their advancement' (Copeland 1988b: 48); 'diverse input and feedback' is about assessing employees' needs directly rather than assuming what they are; and 'self-help' is about encouraging the development of support networks. Responsibility for these changes and their success rests with line managers.

There does appear to be a move away from the conventional approach to equal opportunities towards initiatives that are more individualistic and line manager based. There does not, however, seem to be any significant change in the ways in which access to scarce resources such as senior jobs should be granted. Initiatives aim to get the best out of people, overcome barriers, and ensure that minorities receive the same advantages previously granted only to the dominant group. It is difficult to see a focus on equality based on difference rather than sameness as a key aspect of this new equal opportunities approach, despite the 'diversity' label.

Instead, at least part of the appeal to organizations seems to come from the compatibility between diversity approaches and some of the ideas that have been characterized as 'new industrial relations' or 'human resource management' (Storey 1992; Sisson 1994b). Conventional equal opportunities approaches are deeply rooted in the old approaches to managing labour in that they are bureaucratic in style and tend to see the workforce as a collectivity. They rely on setting rules for managers to follow and on policing whether or not they do so. In contrast, human resource management stresses the role of the individual and the importance of involvement and commitment. An approach based on diversity fits much more comfortably with this style than conventional approaches to equal opportunities, since it recognizes differences within the workforce and sees it as the responsibility of the individual to grasp opportunities offered by an empowering organization. 'This vision sidesteps the question of equality, ignores the tensions of coexistence, plays down the uncomfortable realities of difference, and focuses instead on individual enablement' (Thomas 1990: 114).

There are other strands to this debate which do seem to challenge the 'sameness' notion of equality in a radical way. Copeland (1988a) argues that the objective is to make people feel comfortable and motivated so that they can work as effectively as possible. The lesson for managers is that people will work better if they do not feel they are being squeezed into a narrow mould. Others have gone further and argued that mixed work teams will understand a wider range of customer needs and hence help the organization to be more competitive (Gordon et al. 1991; Greenslade 1991).

In the area of women and management this type of argument blurs into one that argues for a new form of homogeneity by claiming that an alternative style of manager will be more appropriate to organizations in the future. A feminine style of managing, different from but superior to men's, is apt to be lauded, and it might be supposed that this development will result in an influx of women into senior positions. However, we should be wary of confusing the so-called feminization of management style with the question of whether women or men are selected to do the job. As we shall see in chapter 3, it is still men who can best lay claim to whatever characteristics are seen as desirable in a manager.

These examples do challenge the equal treatment model. People may not want to be treated the same with respect to all aspects of their work lives. Instead they might value different working arrangements, or benefit packages, and by successfully managing diversity employers might expect to benefit. What is less clear is what is being said about the basis on which access to scarce resources (such as a job) should be decided. If it is true that a job can be done successfully in a number of different ways, how should candidates be compared? On the equal treatment model, equality is ensured by developing job criteria against which all candidates can be judged without regard to their gender. For the diversity model to be able to defend a different kind of fairness, it would seem necessary to develop some way of comparing approaches that are different but equivalent. There is little explicit discussion of this issue in the diversity literature.

The problem is that apparently progressive ideas like recognizing diversity can actually undermine the proposition that women as a group are the targets of discriminatory practices. There appears to be a shift in the discourse on managing diversity away from any sense that specific groups experience 'disadvantage'. Liff (1996) argues that the version of managing diversity that is most likely to appeal to organizations in the current climate is one that will result in *dissolving* differences rather than *valuing* differences.

The contrast can be described in the following terms. On the one hand, *valuing* diversity approaches are ones which focus on gender differences and see the need to recognize and adapt to them to ensure that women are not disadvantaged. On the other hand, the *dissolving* differences approach focuses on individual differences. It recognizes differences within the workforce and sees all employees as 'different'. Equality, if it is seen as an issue at all for this model, resides in tapping employees' distinctive skills to the full and rewarding them in ways that fulfil their distinctive needs. This model denies the existence of systematic disadvantage based on social differences and implies that equality can be achieved by treating everyone as ungendered individuals. Like the equality policies discussed above, managing diversity does not seek to change the nature and order of jobs and occupations. Rather it encourages a wider range of people to be able to fit into conventionally structured positions.

In the current economic climate, where management ideas about the importance of decentralized organizations, teamworking and innovation predominate, it is this individualized version of managing diversity that is likely to prevail. 'Those concerned about gender equality should be anxious about such a development . . . It allows for individual difference but has no strategy for dealing with the ways in which job structures and personnel practices have been shown to systematically disadvantage women, ethnic minorities and others and to advantage white males' (Liff 1996: 22–3). There can be little wonder that many feminist writers concerned about women's equality have been extremely cautious about recent approaches based on the acknowledgement of difference.

Sameness, Difference and Equality

The extent to which women are the same as or different from men, and the political consequences of making such an assumption, have been much discussed. As mentioned earlier, a considerable amount of feminist theory has agonized over essentialism and criticized liberal equal opportunity programmes for targeting a homogenizing category of 'women'. These theorists have rightly pointed out that the category of 'women' is only constructed in relation to the category of the other. We understand male and female characteristics in relation to each other rather than as independent categories. Indeed, the construction of women as different from men (taken as the measure) is one of the mechanisms whereby male power is maintained. To engage in a dialogue about gender difference within gendered hierarchical workplaces is highly problematic since there is an inexorable tendency for difference to be evaluated as inferior.

At the same time many feminist theories of difference are not particularly helpful for analysing the particular set of problems we have already drawn attention to and will encounter further in this book. The recent feminist theory that draws on deconstructivist ideas has rejected any attempt to define an identity for women as a group

(Nicholson 1990; Scott 1988; Young 1994). Instead, it highlights differences within the categories of women and men (rather than between them) and recognizes other identity categories such as ethnicity. The presentation of a single binary division between men and women simultaneously polarizes the difference between them and exaggerates the homogeneity of each category. As such, the common concerns of, say, black men and black women are obscured, while those of black and white women are exaggerated. This emphasis on different kinds of women with distinctive problems does highlight the limitations of the concept of 'women's needs' embodied in equal opportunity programmes. These feminist notions of equality through difference parallel the shift in equality policy towards managing diversity.

However, simply drawing attention to differences among women does not by itself guarantee a progressive outcome. Too much emphasis on difference between women can lead to the disintegration of the category 'women' and make it harder to understand how women's collective disadvantage is institutionalized at work. On the other hand, too much emphasis on sameness can lead to the uncritical reproduction of the male norm. Politically, therefore, we cannot avoid using the concepts of sameness and difference. In particular, some understanding of the ways in which women are different from men is necessary in order to understand the gender construction of workplaces.

I have attempted to show here that, in practice, workplace equality initiatives have always invoked both sameness and difference. Even when reforms have been constructed primarily around granting equality to women who could prove that they were the same as men, they have left space for claims on the basis of women's difference. The problem is that there is only limited evidence that the policy initiatives from either perspective have led to a reduction in inequality between men and women. Several researchers have found that organizational structures have either been unaffected, or have adapted and incorporated such policies with no significant changes to the gender hierarchy of organizational positions (Bacchi 1996; Cockburn 1991; Dickens 1994; Halford 1992; Shaw and Perrons 1995). The limits to both sameness- and difference-based initiatives have led much contemporary feminist thought to critique or 'destabilize' this binary opposition, and to a growing interest in moving beyond these divisions (Barrett and Phillips 1992; Hirsch and Keller 1990).

Can those who suggest we go beyond sameness and difference offer a better way forward? Scott (1988: 172) argues that 'the only response is a double one: the unmasking of the power relationship constructed by posing equality as the antithesis of difference, and the refusal of its consequent dichotomous construction of political choices.' What this seems to involve in practice is a stress on the multiple identities shared by people, both men and women. Taken to its logical conclusion this approach denies any intrinsic coherence to the category 'women', or, for that matter, any other socially constructed category. So it is far from clear what the gender equality project would mean once the structural inequality on which it is founded has been undermined.

The fundamental problem with this position is that gender is not just a characteristic which divides people into two categories, 'men' and 'women'. Rather, societies are organized through sexual difference and each sex is assigned its own tasks, identities, responsibilities and roles. It is important to stress that the basis of men's power is not simply a product of the ideas we hold and the language we use, but of all the social practices that give men authority over women. Managers' perceptions of job requirements and procedures for assessing merit have been shown to be saturated with gendered assumptions. How will this be changed by the discursive deconstruction of the category of gender? Feminists can argue (as they have for years) that not all women get pregnant, but it seems unlikely that this observation will stop managers thinking 'yes, but no men will.'

In the course of this research I became frustrated with current feminist theorizing about whether we should aspire to equality, to difference, or to a deconstruction of the dichotomy. These debates leave unresolved many of the questions raised by my study of the gender relations of management. The way to emerge from the circularity of sameness and difference approaches is to recognize that, while we must keep both these concepts in play, we need to concentrate on the fact that women workers are disadvantaged. The issue is not that we are different but that this difference is the basis for the unequal distribution of power and resources. As Bacchi (1996) has demonstrated, feminists have been forced into lengthy debates about the ontological status and content of the category 'women' precisely because those in power demand that women justify their claim to categorical recognition. Definitions of 'women' are by their nature political. Men are not called upon in the same way to justify their privilege. Numerous feminist authors have noted that 'man' remains the 'unmarked standard' in discussions about the woman question, while political discourse allows men to represent themselves as people, humanity, mankind. Women are marked as 'gendered', the ones who are different, the other.

This convention can be seen in employers' adoption of 'family friendly' policies which, although gender neutral in form, in fact target women. In response to feminist argument that men as well as women should be encouraged to take time off to look after their children, that it is not women's biological destiny to care for children, progressive employers have adopted a range of 'family friendly' policies. They consist of parental leave entitlements, career breaks, part-time or reduced hours of work, and various forms of childcare support, including on-site services and allowances to subsidize workers' own arrangements (Brannen et al. 1994). Arguing for parental rather than simply maternity leave is designed to promote changes in gendered family roles. However, it conveniently ignores the fact that it is primarily women, though importantly not all women, who require such time off.

The gender-neutral language of parental leave obscures the fact that present social arrangements for care benefit men. The male model of work prescribes full-time and continuous work from the end of education until retirement, with no concessions to the demands of family. Family-friendly policies primarily focus on allowing women to combine family and labour market responsibilities. Their purpose is to enable women to enter and remain in a workforce constructed by men for men without family involvement. The fact that men are also parents is incidental to these reforms. Furthermore, career women are well aware that taking up these leave entitlements serves to confirm men's view that women as a sex are not suited to managerial work. Not surprisingly, senior women managers tend not to have children, as we shall see. Policies that increase support for women's mothering role help to perpetuate the domestic definition of women workers.

One way of highlighting gender privilege is to imagine a form of equality based on a sameness on women's terms, that is to redefine the standard in terms of women's needs and interests (Liff and Wajcman 1996). It is difficult to conceive of 'gender neutral' conditions because we are not used to seeing current institutions as male gendered. So in practice the development of new approaches may involve privileging the female gender. Adopting this strategy enables one to see how male work patterns marginalize women both discursively and materially. 'A social model which *includes* women in the human standard could [make it] possible to speak about women as women, in their own right, and not as "not men"' (Bacchi 1990: 266, emphasis in the original). Using this model, we can retain the category of women but move it from the wings to centre stage.

To take a very practical example of the effect of structuring work around women's needs, think about toilet facilities. This issue is one the author was forced to ponder when confronted by the lack of women's toilets at Cambridge University. As the first woman research fellow in an all-male college, I had to be assigned a secretary's office because it was the only office with access to a ladies' toilet. This example may seem frivolous, but even in the late 1970s serious debate could still be heard about the impossibility of allowing women into male colleges, because women had supposedly fundamentally different toilet requirements.

There are several possible responses to this issue. The solution most frequently adopted is to build additional but separate toilets for women, leaving the men's toilets as they are. However, a more radical solution would be to redesign toilets so that they were no longer gender specific. After all, in private households bathrooms are routinely shared by women and men. It is only in the public sphere that we have grown accustomed to toilets being segregated by sex. Providing gender-neutral toilets in the public sphere would be the equivalent of modelling all toilets on the current female version. As I have written elsewhere, gender relations are embodied in the built environment just as they are embodied, albeit in a less concrete form, in assumptions about work (Wajcman 1991). Work environments, as this example illustrates, both shape and are shaped by ideas about sex differences.

Let us return to our concern with paid work itself. The way that 'full-time' work as currently defined structures most work opportunities clearly reflects the dominance of the male model: it is very difficult to combine such work with domestic commitments. Admittedly, these arrangements mirror expectations about men rather than the interests and needs of all men. It could be argued that the opportunity to work full-time or part-time, an aspect of progressive equality programmes, appears to recognize different needs. However, by leaving full-time work as the dominant option even these programmes construct part-time work not merely as different but also as inferior. Rethinking work from women's perspective could involve prescribing equal working hours for men and women that are compatible with domestic responsibilities.

In the next chapter we will see that the concept of a career is also

based on men's life experience and needs, and premised on a separation between the public and private spheres. The conventional bureaucratic career is built on uninterrupted service to an employer,
often involving geographical mobility as part of career advancement.
Some women are now included in the managerial career but only on
the condition that they can 'take it like a man' and thus minimize
disruption to traditional work regimes. Women are then treated as
'potential men' and entrenched career structures which exclude
employees fulfilling their family and other social responsibilities
remain intact. This pattern is characteristic of the managerial career
which, as we shall see, still presumes the availability of a wife's
domestic services at home. Extremely long working hours mean that,
as well as having to conform to the male model of work, women
managers have to adopt masculine patterns of (non)participation in
the household.

There is a template for employment shaped around the 'typical
circumstances of white, able-bodied men, within organizations where
the culture, norms, values, notions of merit, formal and informal
structures all reflect their attributes, needs, work and life patterns'
(Dickens 1994: 288). It is against this template that those seeking to
get in and get on are measured. Rather than changing individuals to
fit the template, the template should be abandoned. A model of
equality in which women have to adapt to pre-existing male norms is
fundamentally flawed. In the following chapters it will become clear
why so few women are able to benefit from liberal policies and
increase their participation in management.

The argument for a different focus, for what has been called by
Cockburn (1989) a transformative strategy, concerned with the
nature, culture, relations and purpose of the organization, should not
be taken as an argument against equal opportunity initiatives. Rather
it is an attempt to explain why such initiatives generally fail to produce substantial change in the aggregate picture of disadvantage and
discrimination, and to indicate the limits of such prescription. The
success of a few women does not change the nature of managerial
power in the workplace.

The seismic shift in thinking that is needed to achieve genuine sex
equality in organizations is well described by Cockburn: 'For women
to escape subordination to men the relationship of home to work has
to change beyond anything yet envisaged in the name of equality
policy. Men have to be domesticated and in the workplace (to use
Joan Acker's phrase) the rhythm and timing of work must be adapted
to the rhythms of life outside' (1991: 97). Only when fathers also take

their parenting role into work, and only when they are equally tied to the clock, will the institutions of work be reshaped.

Conclusion

In the late 1990s, after many years of equality policies in the workplace, it is often said that we live in a post-equal opportunities world. The implication is that women now compete on equal terms with men. It was the purpose of the research on which this book is based to explore the extent to which workplace equality policies and practices do actually make a difference for women and men managers in organizations today. Certainly the formal implementation of equality policies is widespread. It is now common for large companies to have sex equality policies in place, and the procedures and rules for recruitment and promotion have been examined and rewritten. As a result, there is much less overt sex discrimination. Consciousness of gender issues has been transformed within companies as well as in the wider world outside.

Conventional equality initiatives, however, have made limited impact on women's share of top positions in the labour market. Multinational corporations continue to be run by men. This outcome is not simply the result of a failure to pursue the reforms with sufficient vigour. Rather, there is a more profound issue arising from the way that the whole project has been conceived. The dominant approach still locates the problem in women and situates men as the unremarkable norm. It does not fundamentally challenge the gendered nature of organizations nor men's power within them. It is still men who have the authority to define what constitutes occupational success, and men who monopolize it.

Even though a male model of management continues to prevail, it is far from static. As we shall see from this study, male organizational culture has not been impervious to change. Just as perceptions of what management is change over time, so too does the content of gender categories. We are no longer dealing with the traditional chauvinist scenario in which men are uncomfortable with women's presence in management, preferring to keep them barefoot and pregnant in the kitchen. Rather, a modernized corporate masculinity may readily accept formal equality for women and even welcome women's presence in their workplaces. Indeed some 'liberated' male executives confess that they are learning from women and adopting a softer management style.

At the same time, however, men may be acting to contain changes in the gender order from 'going too far'. Male power is not dying out. It is being reconstituted in a new form. There are emerging signs that the new gender regimes are oppressive to women in their own way. As Pateman (1989) has argued in relation to the modern welfare state, committed as it is to equality for all citizens, contemporary patriarchy is all about the subordination of women within the framework of equality.

A central theme of this book is the extent to which senior women managers are the same as or different from male managers in equivalent posts. There are many protagonists for either position. Again, we will see that this polarity does not capture the complexity of their position. In order to succeed, women are compelled to deny aspects of themselves and to become more like men. However, systematic inequalities between men and women ensure that their experience as managers cannot be the same. Women are constituted as different kinds of workers because of their relation to the domestic sphere and because their bodies are sexualized to a degree that men's bodies are not. The exercise of power by women is rarely seen as legitimate. Yet power is what management is all about. Women thus enter at their own risk, always precariously negotiating the contradiction between being a manager and being a woman. The processes through which organizations and the managerial job are constituted by gender is the subject of ensuing chapters.

2

The Gender Relations of Management

There is now a growing awareness among sociologists, economists and industrial relations, organization and management theorists that the gender of employees and managers does matter. After all, the decline in manufacturing and the growth of services has been predicated on the changing relation of men and women to paid employment. The effects of economic and social restructuring currently occupy a pivotal role in research in the social sciences. The rise in male unemployment and redundancy, women's increased labour force participation and the increasing numbers of women gaining access to managerial and professional employment has led to much speculation, not only about the implications of these changes for the labour market, but also about their implications for family and marital relationships, the nature and organization of domestic work, household finances, lifestyles and consumption patterns.

Despite the rapid growth of women in professional and managerial jobs, and the significant changes that have occurred in the nature of women's careers, the distribution of power, income and overall access to society's resources remains markedly gendered. Sex segregation in labour markets, industries and occupations, and the associated inequality in pay and conditions, have been thoroughly documented (Reskin and Roos 1990; Rubery 1992). The most powerful organizational positions are almost entirely occupied by men. The resilience of men's monopoly on power, pay and status in the face of women's recent entry into their ranks as senior managers has led to increasing interest in how women at higher levels in organizations fare.

The media are fascinated by powerful women, by women cast as pioneers in the corridors of power – sometimes as trail blazers for other women, sometimes as lone rangers pursuing purely personal goals. Most of the academic writing on this theme has been within the mainstream management literature and there has been some reluctance on the part of feminist sociologists studying women and work to delve into it. As privileged individuals who have competed successfully in a man's world, women managers have not been feminism's favourite daughters. The more pressing problem for feminists, and for sociologists, has been to research the continued prevalence of low pay for women's work, the persistence of gender segregation in the labour market, and the concentration of women in undervalued part-time work. Indeed, one of the paradoxical outcomes of increased female workforce participation is a growing divergence within the female labour force, especially between women in low-paid part-time or casual work and those in continuous full-time occupations (Dex 1987; Rubery 1995; Hakim 1993). A similar situation of class inequality among men has long been recognized.

However, as Coyle observed some time ago, 'whilst management is the site of decision-making and power, we [feminists] cannot afford to ignore it' (1989: 119). More recently, women managers have been seen as a symbol and measure of organizational change, an indicator of the success of equality policies. The presence of women in senior management positions is perceived as a more direct challenge to male power within organizations, and as a beacon of hope for all women of change from the top down.

Indeed, because of the enormous power held by senior managers and executives, gender inequalities in access to authority constitute a key mechanism sustaining gender inequalities in workplace outcomes in the economy at large. 'The underrepresentation of women in positions of authority, especially high levels of management, is not simply an *instance* of gender inequality; it is probably a significant *cause* of inequality' (Wright and Baxter 1995). If, as will be argued here, male managers in a male-dominated hierarchy are likely to act in ways that preserve male privileges and advantages, then gender inequality in workplace authority becomes a key institutional element in the reproduction of gender inequality throughout work organizations.

The predominance of men in top management jobs is now well documented. In an extensive study using data from 533 UK-based companies for the years 1989 to 1992, Gregg and Machin (1993) found that 92 per cent of top executives are male. Their relative share rises dramatically as one moves towards the peak of the corporate hierarchy. Men earn significantly more than women for the same jobs, with the largest pay gap at the extreme reaches of the corporate structure. This pay gap is likely to worsen as performance or incentive payments become more common (Kessler 1994). The 1995 National Management Salary Survey (Institute of Management) actually recorded a slight fall in the number of women managers, from 10.2 per cent in 1993 to 9.8 per cent in 1994. This proportion shows a considerable variation in employment by function, with women most concentrated in personnel and marketing and least represented in research and development, manufacturing and production. There is also considerable variation by sector, with women better represented in banking, finance and insurance. The small numbers of women, particularly at the most senior levels, and their recent downward trend, are recorded in the US, Canada, Europe and Australia (Fagenson 1993).

Men's continuing monopoly of upper-level management is even more striking in the United States, where women have made dramatic inroads into management occupations. In 1980 and 1990, respectively, women claimed 30 per cent and 40 per cent of the jobs classified as managerial, executive, and administrative (US Bureau of Labor Statistics, 1991). There are now far more women managers than there are women lawyers, doctors, architects, computer specialists, engineers and natural scientists combined, even though large numbers of women have entered each of these fields in recent years. However, only 5 per cent of senior executives are women, a percentage which has hardly changed in the last decade. Several recent quantitative analyses of the more equitable representation of women in managerial jobs conclude that there is still a significant gender gap in access to decision-making authority and earnings (Jacobs 1992; Reskin and Ross 1992; Wright and Baxter 1995). Despite the feminization of managerial work and federal anti-discrimination regulations, 'women managers were concentrated near the bottom of chains of command; they tended to supervise workers of their own sex, consistent with conventions that women should not supervise men; they were substantially less likely than men to exercise decision-making authority; and their involvement in decision-making was largely confined to offering input into decisions that men made' (Reskin and Ross 1992: 359). Women are still not hiring, firing, and authorizing promotions and pay rises. The same authors are forced to conclude that: 'Although women have made revolutionary gains in access to managerial titles, our findings suggest that the desegregation of managerial occupations has not signaled the decline of sex discrimination in the allocation of workplace authority' (p. 361).

This chapter will examine the most common explanations for women's underrepresentation/men's overrepresentation in senior management. I will begin by considering theories which focus on individual sex differences and then turn to more sociological approaches focusing on the family/work interface and the domestic division of labour. Explanations for the existing pattern of gender segregation in employment have usually been divided into two broad categories: those which derive from the sexual division of labour in the family and those which derive from the organization of employment itself.

It is important to recognize that gender regimes (institutionalized power relations between men and women) in the home and the workplace are not independent of each other, but rather are interdependent and constructed in relation to each other. I will argue that the very idea of a 'worker' is gendered by the marriage/sexual contract which constrains the ability of women to freely exchange their labour power in the same way as men. Current gender arrangements in the family mean that, no matter how similar they are in background and qualifications, men and women enter the labour market as different sorts of workers. In this sense, men as men are much more favourably positioned in the managerial labour market. At the same time, recent feminist analysis has focused on the ways jobs, occupations and organizations are themselves gendered, and on the construction of masculinity and femininity at work. I will therefore examine the processes and practices of gendering within the organization that marginalize and exclude women from management and shore up men's power in the workplace.

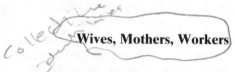

Wives, Mothers, Workers

Individual sex differences

Some of the reasons for women's low representation and the lack of change in a whole range of occupations are well rehearsed. Perhaps the most common explanation is that women themselves lack the necessary attributes to succeed in management. According to human capital theory, the dominant theory a decade ago, wages are a return on investments in human capital because of the direct relationship between human capital and marginal productivity. Individuals make investments in their potential productive capacity (human capital) such as education, training and work experience, which in turn increase their productivity and so their wages. Because women's primary orientation is to their childrearing role they voluntarily choose to invest less in education and training than do men (Becker 1985). They therefore tend to lack the professional qualifications and experience that have become increasingly necessary for promotion to senior positions. Wage differences between men and women, on this view, are due to deficiencies in their stock of human capital, and, ultimately, their lower productivity.

According to this theory, one would predict that as young women achieve entry into junior management and professional posts, it is simply a matter of time before they work their way to the top. In other words, many commentators presume that sex inequality in the labour market will be overcome by the next generation.

However, many studies show that human capital cannot adequately explain differences in pay and authority between men and women (Gregg and Machin 1993; Korenman and Neumark 1992; Waldfogel 1997). Although women's and men's tertiary education, occupational aspirations and attachment to the labour force have become much more similar, the gender gap persists. Moreover, there is some evidence that women need to have higher levels of human capital than men in order to be promoted (see Olson and Becker 1983). Similarly, a British report found that the underrepresentation of women in senior positions is not likely to be ameliorated over time, because the probability of promotion is no higher (and sometimes significantly lower) for women in top executive positions. Contrary to conventional wisdom, the authors demonstrate that the barriers to women's promotion do not result from the occupational segregation of women and men, that is, from the crowding of women into certain occupations. They conclude: 'We can find no evidence that the glass ceiling is cracking in corporate Britain' (Gregg and Machin 1993: 18).

Other more psychologically based theories focus on sex differences in personality traits, cognition, behaviours and individual attitudes towards the job (Hennig and Jardim 1979; Davidson and Cooper 1992). According to this perspective, whether as a result of biology or socialization, men better suit the demands of the managerial role because they possess characteristics like drive, rationality, competitiveness and independence. Women, by contrast, display feminine patterns of behaviour ill-suited to the managerial role as presently constituted. In addition, sex-role socialization leads women to value motherhood and other nurturing types of roles, rather than committing themselves to careers and organizations in the style of top male executives.

As I will detail in the next chapter, most of the psychological research on sex difference is based on laboratory studies which suggest much greater sex difference than research conducted in the field. Careful reviews of these studies indicate their findings should be treated as tentative, at best (Fagenson 1986; Powell 1993). Since these theories do not consider the organizational or societal context to be relevant, they fail to measure the factors that may be responsible for the gender differences actually observed. Moreover, as I will show, when male and female managers are matched for education and organizational level, few differences in performance are in fact found. What is found however, is an enduring perception that women are less likely to possess the key qualities required for management.

The salience of family life

In all these different explanations, the focus is on the individual characteristics of women as the major determinants of career progression. These characteristics are interpreted as the consequence of prior orientations, values or attributes that women import into and express within their paid employment. Dominant sociological approaches also focus on factors outside the workplace, but locate the explanation in family structures and the domestic division of labour.

Within the mainstream sociology of work there is a long history of claims about gender differences in motivation, aspiration and commitment to work (Purcell 1988). Women are seen as regarding their home role as primary and paid work as secondary. When they do engage in paid work, they are perceived as having a lower commitment to it and as being less interested in career advancement than men (Myrdal and Klein 1956). On this view, women's childbearing role and consequent patterns of work have not equipped them for a career in management.

This well-worn theme has been given a recent rerun in the *British Journal of Sociology* (1995–6), where Hakim once again argues that women's commitment and orientation to work differ from men's. While some women do exhibit strong commitment to their careers, other women 'transfer quickly and permanently to part-time work as soon as a breadwinner husband permits it, choose undemanding jobs "with no worries or responsibilities" when they do work, and are hence found concentrated in lower grade and lower paid jobs which offer convenient working hours with which they are perfectly happy' (Hakim 1995: 434). Hakim's intention is to show that much of what has been interpreted by feminist scholars as the effects of sex discrimination is actually the result of women's personal choices. By emphasizing women's attitudes and orientations to work, she ends up blaming women themselves for their inferior position in the workforce.

The basic flaw in this kind of analysis, as many feminists have argued for a long time, is the simplistic fashion in which the notions of choice and commitment are deployed (Wajcman 1981; England 1982). Women working part-time may well express greater commitment to families than full-timers, but this preference is likely to reflect differences in family situation. To understand why women make the 'choices' they do, and how their attitudes are formed, we need to examine the practical and financial constraints which condition their lives. For example, the lack of flexible, affordable childcare remains a major obstacle. It may be more fruitful to consider people's orientation to paid work as fluctuating over their life course, depending on their changing situation. The notion of 'commitment' implies that the 'choices' made by married women – such as whether to work part-time or full-time or at all – are a matter of unconstrained will, rather than being heavily conditioned by structured social arrangements that impose limits on what women can do. This is illustrated in the case of the managers I studied. As I show in the following chapters, I did not find substantial sex differences in commitment to work among managers in my study.

An underlying problem with much of the literature on the salience of family life for women is that it tends to explain women's relation to employment as derived solely from their domestic and family experiences. At the same time, men's relationship to work is seen as having little connection with domestic and family life. This problem is reflected in equal opportunity policies, which have been largely preoccupied with enabling women to combine family duties with a career, as if there is no need for adjustments to allow men to accommodate parenting responsibilities.

Presuming a home/work division in the analysis of employment has led to certain factors being defined as appropriate in the study of either women's work or men's, but not in both (Feldberg and Glenn 1984). The 'job model' has linked men's work attitudes and behaviour to their occupational experiences, while the 'gender model', invoked only for women, links their employment relations to their family experiences. This model treats the position of women in employment as deviant from a male standard. By definition, only women experience conflict between their two roles. Critics of conventional analyses now recognize that, just as women's work cannot be fully understood using a gender model, men's relation to work cannot be understood in isolation from their domestic position. Rather, we need to look at the interrelationship between home and work life as experienced by men as well as women.

The sexual contract

Recent feminist theory has provided a more thoroughgoing critique of the work and home, and the public and private, divide by arguing that the capitalist labour market is itself fundamentally structured by patriarchal relations within the family. Men and women do not enter the labour market on the same terms. Women enter the workplace defined as family-oriented persons, whereas when men enter the workplace, they are stripped of any domestic identity. In her influential text *The Sexual Contract*, Pateman argues that men are in a privileged position to contract out their labour power because the marriage contract frees them from domestic responsibility. Indeed, the employment contract presupposes this sexual contract. 'The attributes and activities of the "worker" are constructed together with, and as the other side of, those of his feminine counterpart, the "housewife"' (Pateman 1988: 135). It presupposes that the worker is a man who has a (house) wife to take care of his daily needs. Thus the very concept of a 'worker' is sex specific, and is constructed in male terms. I will argue that this construction is particularly evident in the case of managerial workers.

My research confirms that men's success is predicated upon the services of a dependent wife. In this respect, Kanter's (1977: ch. 5) classic description of the corporate wife is of continuing relevance (see also Pahl and Pahl 1971). She describes the way in which large organizations assume a 'two-person single career' in which wives are incorporated into their husbands' careers. Value is attached to the wife's role in sustaining her husband's motivation and commitment to the job, leading to the preferential treatment of the 'stable and mature family man'. Although only the man is officially employed by the company, the corporate wife also has a 'career' of sorts, shadowing that of her partner. As husbands move up the management ladder, their wives move from a concern with the boundaries of inclusion and exclusion at junior levels to the representational responsibility of the senior years. According to the bureaucratic theory of the modern corporate organization, 'men were presumed to leave their private relationships at the door to the company when they entered in the morning', but as Kanter shows, husbands and their employers benefit directly from wives' unpaid social and domestic work (1977: 104).

Women are not free wage earners in the same way as men, because prior demands are made on their labour, especially in the family. As a result women do not own their labour power in the same way as men and are unable to sell their labour at the same rate as men. There is now an extensive body of research documenting, as Adkins notes, 'the various ways women are not free to exchange their labour with employers on the same terms as men due to the non-ownership and appropriation of their labour in the family, and the fact that as women they can never have the back-up provided by a wife' (1995: 43). There is no 'corporate husband' role equivalent to that of the corporate wife. Career women, especially in managerial ranks, do not have the advantage of being seen as bringing two people to their jobs. On the contrary, women are seen as bringing less than one full worker.

It is crucial to Pateman's analysis of the sexual contract that women entering the labour market do so with their wage labour power diminished by domestic work. Only men can be 'free' workers on the basis of their control and appropriation of women's labour within marriage. I should emphasize at this juncture that throughout the book I make use of the notion of the sexual contract in two ways. First, I use 'sexual contract' quite literally to refer to the empirical situation whereby becoming and functioning as an employee or a worker requires domestic servicing, or, to put it simply, a wife. Second, I use the notion to refer to the ways in which the sexual contract is a premise built into the fabric of the labour market itself. The social construction of 'jobs' already has within it the assumption that workers will be men and that these men will have wives to take care of their daily needs. These two understandings of the sexual contract come together and find expression in this study both in how the job of 'manager' is revealed to be constituted in male terms with assumed domestic servicing, and in its account of how the sexual contract is lived out day by day. Most senior managers are men who are dependent on domestic servicing.

What implications does this theory have for women managers? To what extent can women compensate for the sexual contract and escape their constitution as 'unsuitable' workers? My research reveals the degree to which women managers are organizing to obtain for themselves the support normally provided by a wife. In order to succeed in the workplace on the same terms as men, senior women managers are contracting out their domestic work. While different groups of women have different experiences of employment, sexual contract theory analyses how all women participate in the labour market on qualitatively different terms from men.

Whatever women do to offload their domestic work, they are still defined in domesticity in a way that men are not. What is problematized at work is *women's* relation to the domestic sphere. 'This is what women *are* to most men (and to most women): people who have domestic ties' (Cockburn 1991: 76). Crucially, the stigma of motherhood affects all women, whether or not they are married and whether or not they have children. For example, employers' perceptions of employees' domestic circumstances affect recruitment and promotion practices. In addition, women are perceived in family roles at work not only because much of their paid work mirrors their domestic roles but also because authority in the workplace is organized around family symbolism and power relations.

So far I have been considering the argument that workers are fundamentally gendered before they enter the labour market. However, gender is not simply an extrinsic attribute which individuals of both sexes bring to the workplace as a fixed component of their identity. Gendered identities are also constructed at work. It is now widely recognized that past attempts to explain gender inequality in employment simply from an analysis of the gendered structuring of the family are limited (Beechey 1987; Walby 1988).

> Precisely because employment relationships are concerned with the distribution of task and authority and these are most often segregated according to sex, the workplace, as the site of tertiary socialization for most people, is the main arena where they learn to play adult gender roles, to develop and modify their performance and interpret the significance of gender in the structure and interaction of the organization and its wider setting. (Purcell 1988: 157)

Differences between women's and men's experiences at the workplace may be just as important as gendered family roles in accounting for differences in their consciousness.

New developments in feminist thinking stress the need to foreground processes or sets of social relations *internal* to the labour market which contribute to the specific construction of women's and men's labour. In fact, it is sometimes difficult to distinguish theoretically between the gender effects of processes internal to the labour market and the indirect effects of domestic responsibilities arising from the sexual division of labour in households. However, the key point is that it is not only people who are gendered. Jobs themselves and organizations are gendered too. The rest of this chapter develops the argument that gender is an intrinsic feature of paid work.

The Gendering of White-Collar Work

Much feminist research has now moved away from explanations in terms of the sphere of reproduction to an examination of how the gender relations of employment are produced at work. There has been growing interest in the ways in which gender divisions are actively created and sustained in the processes of organizational life. In particular, researchers have asked how ideas of masculinity and femininity are constructed at work and how jobs themselves are sex-typed.

Out of a dialogue between feminist theory and organization theory, a concern with the way in which organizations are themselves gendered has emerged. This body of work links gender and organizational analysis, and explores how the male culture of organizations shapes gender relations at work (Acker 1990; Cockburn 1991; Hearn and Parkin 1987; Savage and Witz 1992). The central argument is that gender relations are constitutive of the structure and practices of organizations and that this is key to understanding how men define and dominate organizations. Gendered processes operate on many institutional levels, from the open and explicit to more subtle forms that are submerged in organizational decisions, even those that appear to have nothing to do with gender. They include the way men's influence is embedded in rules and procedures, in formal job definitions and in functional roles. Several themes are emerging from this literature, and I outline those most relevant to understanding the gender relations of management.

The development of bureaucracy and the managerial function

All attempts to theorize modern complex organizations still have Weber's ideal model of bureaucracy at their core. Bureaucratic organizations are based on a clear-cut hierarchy of authority, functional specialization, impersonality, and the impartiality of rules. Written rules govern the conduct of officials at all levels of the organization.

These officials work full-time for a salary and are expected to make a career within the organization. For Weber, writing at the turn of the century, bureaucracy is a progressive moment in that it breaks down old patriarchal structures and removes the arbitrary power held by fathers and masters in traditional society. It ushers in a separation between the activities of the official within the workplace and life 'outside'. This distinction between public and private spheres is what distinguishes bureaucracy from traditionalism. The development of rational-legal authority can be seen as a most efficient way of coping with the administrative requirements of large-scale, complex social systems.

The formal relations of authority described in Weber's ideal-type of bureaucracy have long been recognized as an incomplete picture of power within organizations. Weber himself was aware of informal networks and patterns of behaviour that operated independently of the formally designated structure of authority and responsibilities. A focus on the formal structures alone will not reveal all the dynamics within an organization nor enable us to explain particular organizational outcomes. An extensive literature demonstrates that organizations can be more accurately understood as politically negotiated orders (Bacharach and Lawler 1980; Clegg 1989). Organizational structures can best be seen as emergent entities resulting from the political decisions of particular actors and interest groups. Power is embedded in routine, taken-for-granted practices and ways of being. Organizations are centrally about the exercise and distribution of power and resources.

However, organizational theorists have generally overlooked the way gender inequality is mapped on to ladders of power and authority. Occupational segregation by sex has been integral to how the hierarchical structures of modern bureaucracies are formed. Feminist analyses have exposed the history of modern organizations as a process of either excluding women or admitting them in strictly subordinate roles. The development of large bureaucracies around the turn of the twentieth century was directly associated with what has been called the 'white blouse revolution', the employment of large numbers of women in low-grade clerical work (Cohn 1985; Kwolek-Folland 1994). When the modern organization came into existence, it depended on cheap female labour and helped define women as workers subordinate to men within the emergent white-collar labour markets. Historical research on the development of various institutions such as the British civil service (Corrigan and Sayer 1985), the Post Office (Zimmeck 1992), and Lloyds Bank (Savage 1992) suggest that the emergence of the bureaucratic career was defined in male terms. The managerial career in these organizations is based on men's experiences, needs and life-cycle patterns, including the prospect of continuous full-time employment.

The creation and maintenance of the 'service class' of managers and professionals depended upon female labour in two crucial ways. In the public sphere, men's promotion prospects assumed a concentration of women in occupations 'supplying the raw material or essential "back-up" services for "service-class" occupations; as, for example, clerks, typists, secretaries and punchgirls' (Crompton 1986: 124). Most organizations operated a strictly gendered division of labour in which women and men were recruited into different grades of employment, with different salary scales and promotion prospects. Many imposed marriage bars on their female workforce, forcing them to retire on marriage and to become full-time housewives. As a result of these direct male exclusionary practices, women were kept out of the managerial class.

The idea of the male career, however, was also dependent on the contribution of women in the private sphere, on the existence of a female 'servicer', typically a wife, who was expected to carry out a range of duties for her husband, freeing him to devote more time to the organization's affairs. The managerial/professional career is a particularly telling example of the dependence of male workers upon their wives' domestic labour because it requires long hours, geographical mobility, considerable preparation for public participation, and high standards within the home. 'Modern bureaucratic hierarchies both helped to construct the idea of the dependent housewife and drew upon this for their own advantage' (Savage and Witz 1992: 12).

It is salutary to remember that the establishment of the managerial function as a distinct role, separate from the ownership of industrial capital, only emerged in the late nineteenth and early twentieth centuries with the growth of the large corporation. This separation of ownership from control paved the way for the dramatic expansion in management this century. Between the censuses of 1911 and 1971 the number of managers and administrators in Britain increased by over 300 per cent and, as a proportion of the total employed population, this occupational category more than doubled in size (Price and Bain 1976). The administration of large-scale bureaucracies seemed to demand personal qualities that differed from the aggressive self-interest of owner-entrepreneurs in traditional small-scale enterprises (Bendix 1966). The idea of management as a highly technical function requiring appropriate levels of education, training and expertise had to be invented, along with the cultivation of a new occupational culture.

Modern management theory can be traced back to the scientific management thesis associated with F. W. Taylor. Scientific management established management as a distinct set of technical functions concerned with organization of work (Braverman 1974). Management became defined as a resource for planning, commanding, co-ordinating and controlling. This idea that the work process must be rationalized through the simplification and standardization of tasks was consistent with Weber's conception of the impersonal, 'passionless' bureaucracy. Early management theory thus fixed 'rational man' at the core of management. In *Men and Women of the Corporation* Kanter argues that the growth of management as a specialized profession and the managerial ideologies which legitimated it were from the outset masculinized and paternalistic.

> This 'masculine ethic' elevates the traits assumed to belong to some men to necessities for effective management: a tough-minded approach to problems; analytic abilities to abstract and plan; a capacity to set aside personal, emotional considerations in the interests of task accomplishment; and a cognitive superiority in problem-solving and decision-making. These characteristics supposedly belong to men; but then, practically all managers were men from the beginning. (Kanter 1977: 22–3)

The human relations theory of management that developed later in the 1930s and 1940s did little to change this masculine image of the manager. The human relations model recognized social and emotional considerations by focusing on the human side of organizations. It revealed the importance of employees' social affective needs and of informal structures, such as the relationships and values that existed within small unofficial work groups. This model also emphasized the importance of participation, communication patterns and leadership style in affecting organizational outcomes. However, as Kanter shows, it did not challenge the image of the rational male manager. Writers on human relations theory distinguished sharply between the managers, who could control their emotions, and the workers, who were governed by emotions and sentiment. The separation between reason and emotion marked off the manager from the rest.

This model also provided a script for women's role in management. If they belonged in management at all, their place was in personnel management. Indeed, women had been pioneers in personnel management, which became a distinct area of managerial expertise in American and British industry in the early years of the twentieth century. The fluctuating fortunes of women in personnel management have coincided, as Legge (1987) has shown, with the changing status accorded to the profession. Before the First World War personnel work was identified stereotypically with female welfare activities. Women dominated the profession. Cast as 'social workers', their tasks were seen as selecting and educating employees, and with providing for their health and safety. Such functions were defined as low status and unimportant relative to central male activities like production and finance. Men began to enter this area only when the emphasis in new management theories shifted personnel concerns from welfare issues to those of efficient labour management. Indeed, throughout the 1920s and 1930s, large companies usually split labour/welfare departments into two divisions, one for men and one for women. This trend continued after the Second World War, and by the 1960s and 1970s personnel management had professionalized and achieved high status and remuneration. Women typically held junior personnel positions. Men monopolized the senior ranks.

Redefining the personnel function as an industrial relations function served to distance it from the 'feminine' welfare function. The emphasis was now on the 'male' activities of negotiation, wage determination and the resolution of industrial disputes. As the personnel function achieved a greater measure of power and came to be regarded as a valid contributor to strategic decision-making, women's influence in such functions declined. As a result, the one area of management that has been the traditional stronghold of women came to be dominated by men.

Organizational structure in corporations

The historical legacy of the developments described above is an institutionalized sexual division of labour within hierarchical organizations. Its reproduction is now part of routine organizational practices. Managerial occupations, which involve the exercise of power and authority within organizations, are sex-typed as male. 'For most of the twentieth century a "masculine ethic" of rationality dominated the spirit of managerialism and gave the manager role its defining image. It told men how to be successful as men in the new organizational worlds of the twentieth century' (Kanter 1977: 25). While this gendering is not immutable, it has certainly proved extremely obdurate over the course of this century. When women tried to enter management jobs, the 'masculine ethic' was invoked as an exclusionary principle.

Clearly there have been major changes in the bureaucratic career, and women are no longer formally excluded from managerial occupations. Indeed, as noted above, there has been a massive entry of women into management and the professions since the 1970s. Kanter's pioneering ethnography about the different experiences men and women have of the modern corporation was written before this expansion occurred. Although she precisely captures the myriad ways that women's careers are blocked, she is optimistic that, given time, women will achieve equality in bureaucratic hierarchies. Writing within a liberal feminist vein, she is concerned to show that women's behaviour and orientations in organizations are much the same as men's. On her account, what first appear to be gender differences are really power differences. 'Differences based on sex retreat into the background as the people-creating, behavior-shaping properties of organizational locations become clear' (1977: 9). For Kanter, it is the job that makes the person, not gender that makes the job. The problems facing women in managerial roles are problems of powerlessness, not sex.

Women's fate in corporations, according to Kanter, can be primarily explained in terms of the structure of organizations. Individuals' positions within the opportunity structures of organization, the amount of power they exert in their jobs and the numerical distribution of women in these positions are the critical variables. Accordingly, the best positions are those which offer job occupants opportunity and power and are held by individuals of the dominant social category (males). Advantageous positions foster attitudes, behaviours and values that propel individuals along the fast track. Disadvantageous positions offer their occupants little power and opportunity, and are held by individuals whose social category (females) are few in number. Individuals occupying disadvantaged positions develop attitudes and behaviours that reflect and justify their placement in these limited advancement slots. As a result, sex differences in attitudes, behaviours and cognitions, such as 'feminine traits', derive from women's disadvantageous positions in the organizational structure rather than from gender.

Kanter's illuminating analysis of the boss–secretary relationship reveals both the strength and weakness of her analysis. She invokes the marriage metaphor of the 'office wife' to characterize this relationship and its three defining elements: secretaries derive their status from their boss; managerial discretionary power over secretaries knows no bounds; and personal loyalty is owed to the boss. In addition, there is an expectation that the boss's emotional needs will be looked after by both the 'office wife' and the real wife. Kanter's portrayal of this key organizational dynamic provides some original insights into women's subordinate position within corporations.

While Kanter's analysis highlights the significance of gender and sexuality, she denies they have any explanatory power. Instead, the secretary's destiny is explained in terms of her job function. Kanter regards the personal boss–secretary relation as a bureaucratic anomaly, a relic of feudal patrimony, and foresees a time when the relationship will succumb to bureaucratic rationalization. If men dominate women in organizations not as men but as incumbents of senior official positions, then inequality will end once women are able to move into these powerful positions.

As several commentators have pointed out, Kanter fails to see that the person and the organizational structure are not independent factors and thus ignores the social context and organizational cultures in which managerial behaviour takes place (Fagenson 1990; Green and Cassell 1996; Savage and Witz 1992). She conceives of the modern bureaucracy as gender neutral and relegates to a footnote the revealing comment that she cannot say what difference it would make to her analysis if a secretary were a man (1977: 309). The question of what the boss–secretary relation might look like if they were both women similarly does not arise for Kanter. As Savage and Witz note, 'a notion of power inequalities as in any way built into the very fabric of gender relations themselves is strangely absent from Kanter's analysis' (1992: 28). The way gender is woven into the very fabric of bureaucratic hierarchy and authority relations remains hidden.

More recently, the boss–secretary relationship has come to be seen not as an archaic form but as a new kind of patriarchal structure, paradigmatic of the centrality of gender and sexuality to all workplace power relations (Pringle 1988: 84). Decades on, with many more women entering management levels but still so few reaching the top, there is clearly a need to look for new explanations. Gender segregation, rather than withering away, has taken on new forms. Much of the feminist literature of the 1980s and 1990s has been concerned to explain these new patterns of segregation, that is, to examine new patriarchal strategies of inclusion and segmentation. In other words, the focus has shifted from women's exclusion from certain occupations (horizontal segregation) to how women are incorporated but segmented within occupations (vertical segregation; see, for example, Crompton and Sanderson 1990; Reskin and Roos 1990; Witz 1992). These new concerns force us to look beyond the formal structure of organizations to the hidden barriers that inhibit women's achievements. The concept of organizational culture has been usefully deployed by feminists to theorize the way in which male power also operates through the discourses and practices that permeate and constitute organizations.

The gendered culture of organizations

At the same time, there has been a resurgence of interest in 'organizational culture' within both mainstream organizational analysis and popular texts, such as *In Search of Excellence* (Peters and Waterman 1982). The current fashion in human resource management, imitating Japanese methods, identifies cultural management as a key element of competitive advantage. The prescription for enhanced performance requires senior managers to create strong corporate cultures to win the commitment, and not simply the compliance, of their employees. This new orientation has led to a vigorous debate in the management literature about how to conceptualize 'organizational culture'.

In an influential paper, Smircich (1983) distinguishes between two broad theoretical approaches. Organizational culture can be conceived as a variable, something an organization *has*, or as something emerging from social interaction, something an organization *is*. In this second version, culture is both produced and reproduced through the negotiation and sharing of symbols and meanings. It is simultaneously the shaper of human action and the outcome of that process. This dynamic concept of culture highlights the limits of managerial power to manipulate cultural change, because ultimately it is not something managers can control. Moreover, a variety of cultures can coexist within a single organization. 'Corporate culture – that shared by senior management and presented as the "official" culture of the organization – may be only one of several subcultures within an organization, and may be actively resisted by groups who do not share or empathize with its values' (Legge 1994: 408). Although neither mainstream nor popular organizational analysis typically address gender issues, it is this same 'socially emergent' view of culture that has been developed by academic feminists and imported into the discourse of equal opportunity policies under the rubric of 'the need for cultural change'.

Current feminist perspectives on women managers attempt to integrate analyses of organizational structures with explorations of organizational cultures. Known as gender and organizational analysis, this approach places patriarchal power relations centre stage (Acker 1990; Calas and Smircich 1992; Cockburn 1991; Green and Cassell 1996; Hearn and Parkin 1987; Mills and Tancred 1992). The main strength of this literature lies in its attention to gendered cultural processes, like the way people talk to each other, how they interact informally and their taken-for-granted assumptions, values and ideas. It is largely through such cultural representations and meanings that people build their understandings of the gendered structure of work and opportunity within organizations. Indeed, organizations are one area in which widely disseminated images of gender are continuously invented and reproduced.

Although there are diverse historical and contemporary expressions of masculinity and femininity, the culture of organizations is predominantly male. This culture, in its symbolic and material aspects, is so ingrained that it is seen as ungendered. The way men generate a masculine culture in and around their work has been written about most extensively in relation to manual and technological workplaces (Cockburn 1983; Wajcman 1991). Women have by and large been frozen out of the shop-floor culture of working-class men, which is based on mechanical skills and toughness. Everything associated with manual labour and machinery – dirt, noise, danger – is suffused with masculine qualities. Machine-related skills and physical strength are fundamental measures of masculine status and self-esteem according to this model of masculinity. In contemporary Western society, hegemonic masculinity, the culturally dominant form of masculinity, is strongly associated with aggressiveness and the capacity for violence, attributes that workplace cultures reflect (Connell 1995). While the nature of managerial work clearly does not require physical prowess, the ethos of masculinity nonetheless resonates among professional middle-class men.

The dominant symbolism of corporations is suffused with masculine images. Success means being lean, mean, aggressive and competitive with tough, forceful leaders. Managerial work itself is conceptualized as involving constant action. A potent image is that of a fire-fighter dealing with constant and unpredictable pressures, with images of doing rather than thinking – a veritable 'action man'. The social construction of management is one in which managerial competence is intrinsically linked to qualities attaching to men. These persistent male stereotypes of management serve to make 'natural', and thereby help to generate, a close identification between men and management. The resulting culture is one that marginalizes women. Women managers are out of place, in foreign territory, 'travellers in a male world' (Marshall 1984).

These images and representations are both cause and effect. Through everyday interaction at work, they reinforce individual gender identities, the gendered sense of self, the identity created and experienced by the individual. However, personal identity is not static, but is constantly created and recreated in social interaction at work, at home, and in other everyday activities. Identity is the end result of a process that evaluates, selects and integrates self-images in response to new experiences.

The idea that identity is fluid and relational is now a common argument in feminist postmodernism, and has also been articulated, in a somewhat different form, in earlier versions of social theory. Butler (1990) has stressed that gender involves a discursive practice or 'performance'. As the symbolic interactionists long ago emphasized (for example, Mead 1934), actors have a unique capacity to monitor their own action reflexively. That is, they can be aware of what they are doing and modify their behaviour in the light of their interpretation of the responses of other people. People use many forms of 'impression management' to ensure that others react to them in ways they wish (Goffman 1969). Consciousness of gender is a constant dynamic of workplace interaction, where part of what men and women learn are scripts for gender-appropriate behaviours and attitudes. Scripts include things like language, clothing and presentation of self as a gendered member of an organization. Such scripts can be extremely complex, since appropriate codes of masculine and feminine style and behaviour differ depending on the type of work performed and the level of particular jobs in the organizational hierarchy. As a consequence, 'some aspects of individual gender identity, perhaps particularly masculinity, are also products of organisational processes and pressures' (Acker 1990: 140).

For most men, gender interaction at work tends to be a positive experience, promoting social and personal integration and confirming male identity rather than generating role conflict and status ambiguity. For most women, who are employed in predominantly female sectors of the labour force, their feminine identity is also reinforced at work. However, women who assume roles and statuses traditionally filled by men find themselves in conflict with prevailing norms. Their presence makes the gendered content of jobs and workplace relations more visible, and their sex subjects them to a scrutiny that is absent when they occupy their 'natural' place in the gender hierarchy.

Sexuality at work

Sexuality, in its diverse forms and meanings, is implicated in these gendered organizational processes. Until quite recently, 'the importance of the sexual aspect of gender has been subsumed within a consideration of power differences, without detailed analysis of how sex, as a component of gender, is mobilized in the exercise and deflection of power' (Purcell 1988: 171). New currents in social theory, much of it influenced by Foucault, have highlighted the connection between gender, sexuality and organizational power, emphasizing the significance of sexuality for employment relations (Adkins 1995; Burrell 1984; Gherardi 1995; Hearn et al. 1989; Pringle 1988).

Ethnographic studies of male-dominated shop-floor culture have revealed that discourses concerning men's sexuality are likely to pervade the workplace (Cockburn 1983; Collinson and Collinson 1989; Willis 1977). In these contexts, male workers bond with each other through sexual banter, creating a solidarity that provides a basis for labour resistance to control by management. It is part of an assertion of the masculinity and power of manual work. Similarly, sexualized social relations are a normal part of the functioning of office work. While pornographic posters are not such a feature of office environments, the new information technologies have provided another medium for men's exchange of sexual fantasies, via the Internet. These forms of workplace sexuality have routinely been interpreted as representing worker resistance.

Reviewing the historical evidence, Burrell (1984) argues that sexuality has been systematically suppressed and eliminated from modern bureaucratic organizations in the interests of production and control. Active sexuality was the enemy of orderly procedures, and excluding women from certain areas of activity may have been, at least in part, a way to control sexuality. Attempts to banish sexuality from the workplace were part of the wider process that differentiated the home, the location of legitimate heterosexual activity, from the place of capitalist production. These twin processes, the eradication of sexuality within and the containment of sexuality outside the work site, continue to influence the lives of workers today. For Burrell, the survival of sexual relations at work therefore represents a major frontier of control and resistance in organizational life. Although he acknowledges that conventional heterosexuality commodifies women as the objects of sexuality, his emphasis is on 'resistance to organizational desexualization'. Sexual relations at work represent a demand not to be controlled by management.

What Burrell fails to acknowledge is that male solidarity is often achieved directly at the expense of women. For men, public expression of sexual behaviour is supposed to be a mark of manhood, whereas for women it is often a form of degradation. Although some women also participate in mock flirtation and sexual banter to alleviate the tedium of bureaucratic control, the interplay of sexuality and gender differences in the workplace more often indicates male attempts to control and restrict women. Feminists have emphasized the link between the dominance of men's sexuality within organizations and their power. Hearn and Parkin (1987) have pointed to the ways in which male managers use sexuality, harassment, joking and abuse as routine means of maintaining authority. Sexual harassment on the job is now widely recognized as a form of sex discrimination. Men use their sexuality to maintain their dominant position, a stratagem that becomes particularly evident when women enter 'male' environments or occupations. Gender interaction at work serves to remind women of their essential marginality and vulnerability in 'male' territory. Accordingly, men's focus on sexuality is 'as much an exercise in power as in sexuality' (DiTomaso 1989: 70).

Organizational cultures contain a variety of sexual discourses that include both a male 'heterosexual subtext' and a male 'homosexual subtext', to use the terms coined by Collinson and Hearn (1994). By this they mean that men sexualize and objectify women in order to maintain women's subordination within organizations. Sexualized social relations, including sexual harassment, sexual banter and heterosexual flirtation, are a normal rather than exceptional part of the functioning of hierarchical organizations. Men's use of women as sexual currency stresses the solidarity of men as well as men's difference from women.

On the other hand, these cultures are also characterized by men's preference for male company, as Kanter (1977) pointed out long ago in her discussion of 'male homosociability'. Practitioners often refer to this cultural dynamic as a 'men's club' which serves to perpetuate women's exclusion from power and influence. Male managers share a common language and understanding with others of their own kind. They feel most comfortable communicating with each other and promote 'clones' of themselves. For women, however, the contradictory demands of being a woman and being a manager are difficult to balance. Their success depends on how well they negotiate their sexuality and manage their 'femaleness'. Their femininity is always a potential obstacle to power.

My central argument is that theorizing male power in organizations involves seeing organizations as arenas of men's sexual dominance. Whether this new focus on sexuality in organizational life has displaced rather than simply enlarged the gender paradigm of organizations is still an open question (Witz 1993). Much recent writing on sexuality and organizations tacitly assumes a Foucauldian concept of power, which treats power as a discursive relation that is always in flux. In contrast to the traditional conception of power as coercion and constraint, this view emphasizes power as a pervasive aspect of all human relationships that is always under negotiation. While adding new insights into how power is exercised and experienced in bureaucratic organizations, this focus on cultural and discursive practices has a tendency to eclipse the systematic nature of 'corporate patriarchy'. It can lead to a preoccupation with cultural processes at the expense of an analysis of the structural conditions in which cultures operate. A central issue is how culture is conceptualized, that is, whether it encompasses institutions, roles, rules, bodies and buildings, as well as how people speak and relate to each other.

A fashionable theoretical move in recent work is to focus on the body and space within organizations. While supposedly giving materiality to sexual power relations, they frequently end up being treated entirely as discourse. The politics of the body is at work in organizations, most obviously in sexual harassment but also in the very nature of so much of women's employment. In particular, various kinds of service work demand a sexualized presentation of the body. Indeed, a common feature of women's paid work involves the sexual servicing of men, such as responding to sexual innuendos and men's advances (Adkins 1995).

Women's bodies are an implicit part of the employment contract. As Gherardi (1995: 42) shows, the employment contract grants employers command over the bodies of their employees, bodies that are sexually differentiated. The sexual skills or services of employees are thereby acquired and incorporated into their organizational role. A prime example is the job of air hostess for which physical appearance and a willing demeanour are essential qualifications. On the other hand, Acker (1990: 152) also emphasizes that women's bodies are often ruled out of order: 'women's bodies – female sexuality, their ability to procreate and their pregnancy, breast-feeding, and child care, menstruation, and mythic "emotionality" – are suspect, stigma-tized, and used as grounds for control and exclusion.' This apparent contradiction is part of the wider story that differentiates women from men and marks their bodies as suitable for different sorts of work. The extent to which the male body is inscribed within the managerial function will be explored in chapter 5.

In this chapter I have rejected a focus on the personal characteristics of women and men managers in favour of an analysis of the sexual contract and the way gender regimes in the home are embedded in the organization of paid work. That is to say, work in industrial societies is structured around a number of gendered assumptions about workers, and about relations between the workplace and life outside it. The notion of a separation between the public and private spheres is itself a patriarchal construction, because it both presumes and privileges men's life experience. Organizations are a crucial site for the ordering of gender and the distribution of power. Indeed, the history of modern organizations has involved a process either of removing women or of admitting them in strictly subordinate roles. The male manager has been constituted as the standard against which women are to be measured and understood as different and deficient. Gender power pervades perceptions of merit, performance, career, choice and authority. The following chapters explore the various practices that establish and foster the gender regime of management. Although a minority of women are now gaining some organizational and economic power, we will see that their presence hardly amounts to a transformation.

3

It's Hard to be Soft: Is Management Style Gendered?

Traditionally, men have been seen as better suited than women to executive positions. The qualities usually associated with being a successful manager are 'masculine' traits such as drive, objectivity and an authoritative manner. Women have been seen as different from men, as lacking the necessary personal characteristics and skills to make good managers. The entry of women into senior levels within organizations over the last decade or so has brought such stereotypes into question. One of the issues generating debate is whether women bring a distinct style of management to organizations as we enter the twenty-first century.

If a participative, cooperative management style is in the ascendancy, this style is more closely associated with women than men. So there is much at stake. Recent developments in organization theory, such as human resource management and Japanese management, have moved away from the hardness of quantitative methods and deterministic conceptions of corporate strategy. According to the new orthodoxy, effective management needs a softer edge, a more qualitative, people-oriented approach. If women really have a 'natural' proclivity for this style, concerns about their career prospects may be misguided. Because they more closely fit the new criteria for success in management, women will flourish as never before.

This chapter examines the thesis that management style is itself gendered. It asks whether there are sex differences in how women and men manage, and what this means in terms of defining the skills necessary for managerial success. My data show that the women who have made it into senior positions are in most respects indistinguishable from the men in equivalent positions. In fact, the similarities between women and men far outweigh the differences between women and men as groups. This finding leads me to argue that there is no such thing as a 'female' management style. However, my data also suggest that gender stereotypes are still deeply entrenched. Despite the current enthusiasm for a 'feminine' style of management, women have to adopt the style associated with male management in order to succeed. Style is after all an intrinsic part of the managerial job which, as I have argued, is itself gendered male.

The 'Feminine' in Management

Recently there has been a positive re-evaluation of gender stereotypes of women managers. This development is due largely to the fact that standard renditions of women's leadership qualities are in tune with current fashions in management theory.

During the 1980s management theory underwent a paradigm shift, reflecting a growing recognition that managerial processes had damaged the competitive position of US business. A central theme has been how to adapt Japanese management techniques to Western economies. Leadership, just-in-time management, teamworking and total quality control all entered managerial discourse alongside more general concerns about flexibility, new technology and niche marketing (see reviews by Wood 1989; and Sisson 1994a). This 'new wave' of management theory criticizes American management practice as placing too much weight on a centrally imposed rationality, expressed through undue emphasis on the measurable, involving the manipulation of complex structures of compliance. In Japanese business, the emphasis is on the creation of a strong cohesive culture of collective commitment to achieve organizational goals. The Americans had neglected this 'transformational' leadership in favour of a shorter-term, 'harder' transactional style. 'The lesson was clear: cultural management that secured the commitment of employees as valued assets – hallmarks of the "soft" human resource management model – should be the order of the day' (Legge 1994: 403). Successful firms are described as people oriented and decentralized, uncluttered by rigidly hierarchical and bureaucratic layers of management. Leadership is now concerned with fostering shared visions, shared values, shared directions and shared responsibility.

In the more popular versions of these new wave theories, gender images are commonly deployed. They are used to suggest that women have a more consensual style of management, and that this will be an advantage in post-industrial corporations. According to management gurus Peters and Waterman (1982), managers need 'irrational, intuitive' qualities for success, qualities that are explicitly described as feminine. They challenge the masculine image of the rational manager by demonstrating that seemingly feminine characteristics are actually potent managerial tools. Similarly, in its report *Management Development to the Millennium*, the British Institute of Management (1994) argues that 'female ways of managing will be more appropriate in the millennium.' In the future, they say, organizations will be less hierarchical, will rely more on teamwork and consensus management, and 'feminine' skills of communication and collaborative working will come to the fore. *Enterprising Nation*, the Report on Leadership and Management Skills published by the Australian government (1995), concurs that managers need to embrace women's 'soft' skills: 'In this new way of managing, increasing recognition is given to factors such as relational rather than competitive values, the need for firms to seek interdependence rather than dominance in the marketplace and for business opportunities to be nurtured in an "emergent" manner through affiliation and cooperation rather than rationality, separation and manipulation' (p. 8). So the advantage men formerly enjoyed in 'command and control' style organizations will pass to women in these new organizations.

This controversy about gendered management style also resonates with key preoccupations of feminist theory, ground traversed in chapter 1. There I reviewed the extensive debate in the feminist movement as to whether women should be seen as essentially different from men or essentially the same. During the 1970s feminist authors often minimized or even denied differences between men and women, in order to argue that women had the same potentialities as men and should have equality of opportunity at work. Since the 1980s, however, many feminist scholars have begun to emphasize women's difference and to celebrate what they see as specifically female values and ways of behaving, feeling and thinking (Gilligan 1982). The new and fundamentally feminist twist in the argument is that difference is no longer equated with inferiority or hierarchical ordering. For example, Ferguson's (1984) radical feminist case against male bureaucracy rests on the assumption that women-centred modes of organization are more democratic and participatory. Questioning whether the aspiration for equality is too limited a goal, such writers claim superiority for women's ways of doing things and are positive about the possibility of social change through the revaluing of gender differences.

The literature on women in management reflects this shifting emphasis. Much of the early research was aimed at discrediting the idea that women themselves lacked the necessary attributes to succeed in management (Hennig and Jardim 1979; Marshall 1984). These critics targeted psychologically based theories which viewed women's personality traits as ill-suited to the managerial role. Studies of women in management using this perspective argued that there were no essential differences between men and women, refuting notions that women are less effective as managers than men.

The feminine stereotype is now being challenged. The debate was sparked off by an article in the *Harvard Business Review* (Rosener 1990), questioning whether women have a different style of management from men, and what its significance might be for management practice in general. Rosener argues that women executives are now making it to the top, 'not by adopting the style and habits that have proved successful for men but by drawing on the skills and attitudes they developed from their shared experience as women . . . They are succeeding because of – not in spite of – certain characteristics generally considered to be "feminine" and inappropriate in leaders' (pp. 119–20). In contrast to the command-and-control leadership style associated with men, she describes women's style as 'transformational and interactive' because they actively encourage participation, share power and information, enhance the self-worth of others and stimulate enthusiasm about work. Loden (1985) and Martin (1993) similarly argue that female managers, because of biology and socialization, are ideally suited to today's decentralized organizations where teamwork and delegation, rather than hierarchy and direction, are the key.

The conclusion drawn in this literature is that, rather than women managers modelling themselves on men, the norm of effective management should be based on the way women do things. Accordingly, men will need to acquire the skills and qualities of 'feminine leadership' if they are to maintain their position. In the words of Tom Peters: 'Gone are the days of women succeeding by learning to play men's games. Instead the time has come for men on the move to learn to play women's games' (Fierman 1990: 71).

Although much of this literature is from the US, it finds a resonance among British feminists, who have embraced this notion of women's different style in response to the limited achievements of equal opportunity policies. They argue that the 'sameness' approach, embodied in equality policies, leads to women succeeding only on men's terms. For example, Ashburner says that 'the consequence of highlighting the differences between men and women, far from further marginalising them, is to challenge the view that women do not conform to the "norm", and to put the emphasis onto the issue of changing management style and structures. Minimising differences avoids any challenge to the predominant male value system' (1994: 193–4). This discussion of women's different style mirrors a shift in the language of equal opportunities from a concern with equality to 'valuing diversity', in this case a valuing of diversity in management styles (Liff and Wajcman 1996).

Managers of Reason

When I reflect on the copious literature on leadership style, I am struck by the way in which it is permeated by gender stereotypical oppositions, such as that between hard and soft, reason and emotion. Instead of challenging the gendered nature of the dichotomies, they simply invert them. Leadership traits that correspond with male traits like dominance, aggressiveness and rationality are now presented negatively, while formerly devalued feminine qualities like the soft and emotional are presented positively. This simple inversion hardly signals a great step forward for women's prospects in management. Have feminist scholars in business schools adopted the correct strategy by embracing these new business fashions and using them to promote the cause of women managers? I have my doubts.

My book *Feminism Confronts Technology* (1991) presents a critical analysis of the way scientific and technological practices are depicted as detached, objective activities appropriate to men. Similarly, the discourse on management rationality has operated to legitimate and normalize masculine authority and to exclude women. In both cases, the central problem is that the patriarchal construction of gendered subjects, of what it is to be a man or woman, continues to be mapped on to a set of symbolic polarities like culture versus nature, mind versus body, reason versus emotion, objectivity versus subjectivity, the public realm versus the private realm, and read in a gendered hierarchy.

For well over a decade, feminist philosophers have exposed the way this symbolic dualism feeds into essentialism, or the assertion of fixed, unitary and opposed female and male natures (Lloyd 1984; Harding 1986). These writers point to the historical specificity of such gender metaphors, in that there is no behaviour or meaning which is universally and cross-culturally associated with, for example, either rationality or intuition. Both 'masculinity' and 'femininity' are socially constructed and are in fact constantly under reconstruction. Furthermore, it must be stressed that the values being ascribed to women originate in the historical subordination of women. The association of women with nurturance, warmth and intuition lies at the heart of traditional and oppressive conceptions of womanhood. They are meanings and values ascribed to women in a world where men are more powerful than women. Definitions of the feminine are profoundly distorted by the male-dominated structure of society.

Feminist organization theorists are seeking to apply this epistemological analysis in their deconstruction of the rational model of management and organizations. Taking issue with the concept of 'bounded rationality', which is often used in organization theory to critique the notion of 'pure rationality', Mumby and Putnam (1992) argue that it too is grounded in male-centred assumptions that exclude alternative modes of organizing. Bounded rationality acknowledges that rationality, typically defined as intentional, reasoned, goal-directed behaviour, is limited by organizational actors and their institutional practices. As these authors point out, however, even this concept of rationality positions other forms of reasoning such as intuition and judgement as non-rational, and decisions based on emotions as irrational. Emotional experience defined as feelings, sensations and affective responses to organizational situations is devalued and marginalized, or treated as inappropriate in the work context.

The merits of Mumby and Putnam's project are summed up thus: 'Deconstructing the dichotomy between rationality and emotionality debunks organizational efforts to reify certain experiences and behaviours as either masculine or feminine' (1992: 480). They contrast bounded rationality with their concept of 'bounded emotionality', which refers to an alternative mode of organizing in which nurturance, caring, community, supportiveness and interrelatedness shape organizational experience. Emotions, then, should be integral to organizations.

These authors recognize that rationality is a social phenomenon in which emotion plays a central role, and draw on the feminist discussion of the knowledge-producing dimension of emotion (Jaggar 1989; Smith 1987). Nevertheless, their work ultimately rests on a gendered conception of emotion. What counts as 'emotion' is still defined within a discourse of gender difference. For them, emotionality constitutes positive feelings of mutual affection, cohesion, interrelatedness, tolerance of ambiguity. They do not see that organizations are already founded on emotion: the emotions of aggression, fear and anxiety, and that 'emotions' may be key in terms of the constitution of gendered management (Jackall 1988; Van Maanen and Kunda 1989). Neither the management literature nor this feminist analysis successfully challenges the dialectic of emotionality and rationality, or considers how such distinctions interrelate with the construction of masculinity and femininity in an organizational context.

A more innovative approach is possible if we turn from asking 'What are the emotions?' to the question 'In what situations and in what ways can the emotions be considered acquired responses, determined by socio-cultural prescriptions and behaviour?' (Gherardi 1995: 153). A sociological perspective shifts attention from emotion as a physiological experience to the learning of the language of emotions, and to the cultural variability of emotions and their expression. That is, emotions can only be understood in their social and institutional context. The same emotions in the public world of work and in the private sphere acquire very different meanings. Being aggressive at home may be defined as being emotional, but being aggressive in the public sphere may be seen as effective leadership. Fundamentally, the terms rational and emotional derive their meaning from their specific connection with the domains of the public and private. The point here is not whether men are necessarily less or more emotional than women, but how these feelings are *expressed, perceived* and *interpreted* within organizations.

To return to the question of leadership style, the central issue is that different interpretations are placed upon apparently identical modes of behaviour. The point at which a decisive move becomes precipitative, or a tactful decision becomes a cave-in, depends on the interpretative framework, not on the behaviour itself. Any action may be interpreted in a radically different way depending on whether the actor is a man or a woman. For example, a particular action or experience might be defined as 'firm', 'decisive' and 'rational' when constructed in relation to a man, and as 'bossy', 'hysterical' and 'irrational' where a woman is involved. A woman exercising a democratic leadership style may be seen as soft or indecisive. The common description of men as more aggressive and competitive managers than women can be recast as a description of men being more emotional than women. Yet uncontrolled competition and aggression are seen as rational when in pursuit of organizational goals. The same leadership behaviour will be interpreted differently depending on the gender of the leader.

This points to a major problem with the leadership literature generally. The central fallacy of leadership studies is that they reduce the study of power and leadership to the individual. Like power, leadership is not simply a trait which people possess. It is a structural asset that is exercised through a social network and is dependent upon the accounts and responses of those who are assessing the actions of a manager in particular situations. My study shows that organizational constraints rather than individual personality traits determine management style.

Many of the ideas canvassed above, particularly in relation to questions of management style and gender difference, have been elaborated in the absence of a firm empirical foundation. A major weakness of the empirical research that does exist is its tendency to treat women managers in isolation from men. The failure to examine the experience of men within the same organization inevitably limits our understanding of how managers are made. This study aims to correct the imbalance by presenting comparative material on the attitudes and experiences of women and men managers. Firstly, I investigate the extent to which female and male managers subscribe to conventional views about women managers. I then go on to consider whether women and men have distinct styles of management, and how managerial stereotypes match with gender stereotypes. I argue that a danger with the recent theoretical turn towards accentuating gender difference is that it may serve to reproduce gender stereotypes and, in doing so, divert attention from continuing sex discrimination in organizations.

Attitudes towards Women Managers

Given the marked increase in women managers in recent years, one might expect representations of the managerial position in terms of gender to have been radically transformed. Studies of the relationship between sex, managerial stereotypes and gender stereotypes were first conducted in the early 1970s in the US. In 1973, Schein reported findings that strongly influenced the thinking of industrial and organizational psychologists working in the area of sex bias and discrimination. Using a 92-item attribute inventory to characterize gender stereotypes, she asked male managers at nine insurance companies across America to characterize 'women in general', 'men in general' and 'successful middle managers'. She found that 'successful middle managers' possessed an abundance of characteristics generally associated with men rather than with women. Moreover, successful managers were viewed as more like men than women in terms of attributes considered critical to effective work performance, such as leadership ability, self-confidence, objectivity, forcefulness and ambition. These results indicated that women were perceived as lacking the qualities essential for success in management positions.

Several studies replicating Schein's research 15 years later by Heilman et al. (1989) demonstrate that managerial stereotypes held by male managers have remained essentially the same. They persist in viewing women in general as far more deficient in the attributes necessary for success as a manager than men in general. Moreover, even with the manager label firmly affixed, women are thought to differ in important ways from men and successful managers, most notably in their leadership ability and business skills, attributes central to managerial performance. The authors conclude that 'assumptions of progress as a result of social, legal, and organizational changes are unwarranted . . . women still appear to be burdened by perceptions depicting them as unfit for effectively enacting the managerial role' (Heilman et al. 1989: 942).

Evidence about women managers' attitudes is less conclusive. Some studies indicate that, unlike women in the 1970s, contemporary female managers do not sex-type the managerial position but view women and men as equally likely to possess characteristics necessary for managerial success (Brenner et al. 1989). Other studies do not find a significant difference between men and women. For example, Powell (1993: 154) reports that in a study of undergraduate business students about 70 per cent of both women and men still described a good manager in predominantly masculine terms. Virtually no one preferred a 'feminine' good manager. In sum, it would seem that men, and to a lesser extent women, continue to describe good managers as being endowed with typical masculine traits rather than feminine traits. Negative images of women managers have deep roots, are widely shared and are remarkably resistant to change.

Given the resilience of sexual stereotypes, it is important to establish what currency they have for the managers in my study. I found no major differences between the views of women and men in response to more general questions about the role of women in management. Asking people to respond to stock statements along a scale is somewhat crude as it may promote conventional answers. However, I included this exercise for comparison with an earlier British survey. The following set of statements mirrors the set asked by Coe in a report on members of the British Institute of Management (1992): 'women managers have positive skills to bring to the workplace'; 'male managers are more committed to the organization than women managers'; 'there should be positive discrimination for women managers'; 'women should not combine a management career and motherhood'; 'all managers should be treated the same, regardless of family responsibilities'; 'I do find it/would find it difficult to work for a woman manager.' The results are set out in table 3.1.

Overall there is not much difference between the views of women and men in relation to these statements, both being overwhelmingly positive about women managers' skills, commitment, and right to combine a career with motherhood. However, as in Coe's survey, some differences emerge at the extremes. Twice as many women as men 'strongly agree' that women managers have positive skills to bring to the workplace; well over twice as many women as men

Table 3.1 Percentage distribution of respondents' attitudes towards women managers

		Strongly agree	Agree	Disagree	Strongly disagree
Women managers	Men	41	56	3	–
have positive skills	Women	80	19	1	–
Male managers are	Men	1	13	65	21
more committed	Women	2	7	39	52
There should be	Men	1	10	45	44
positive discrimination	Women	2	10	56	32
Women should not	Men	1	10	51	37
combine career and motherhood	Women	–	3	35	62
All managers	Men	38	47	12	2
should be treated the same	Women	42	39	17	2
Difficult to work	Men	1	9	49	41
for a woman manager	Women	1	3	42	54

'strongly disagree' that male managers are more committed to the organization than women; a higher proportion of women 'strongly disagree' with the statement that women should not combine a management career and motherhood; and men are more likely than women to 'strongly disagree' with the statement that there should be positive discrimination for women managers. In fact, there is very little support for positive discrimination among men or women.

In answer to a separate set of questions about preferences for male or female managers they work *with* or *for*, most men and women express no preference. In addition, most respondents (86%) say that neither men nor women make better managers. In this context it is worth noting that 45 per cent of the managers report that they have actually worked for a woman manager, with a slight tendency for women to report it more.

However, in sharp contrast to these views, when respondents were asked whether they would prefer to work for a manager of their own sex, a sizeable proportion (21%) of men say that they would prefer to work for a male manager. In the words of one male respondent, who had himself never worked for a female manager, his preference is still for a male boss: 'it's just a comfort zone thing.' Interestingly, 10 per cent of women also say that they prefer to work for male managers. Neither men nor women express a preference for a woman manager. This would indicate that women are still far from being fully accepted in senior management positions.

Managing to Differ?

Claims about women and men having distinct styles of management are difficult to investigate empirically, let alone substantiate. A comprehensive review of this research, most of which is North American and is set largely within a social psychological perspective, is provided by Eagly and Johnson (1990). They demonstrate that most of the evidence for sex differences in leadership style is derived from two types of study, namely laboratory experiments and assessment studies. The data usually come from responses to fixed-choice questions, such as whether leaders have a task-oriented versus an interpersonal style, or a directive versus a participative style. The subjects are either college students or people not in management positions. They are typically placed in artificial environments; and they interact as strangers on a short-term basis, without the constraints of established organizational roles. Consequently, they evince great ambiguity about how to behave. Gender expectations may provide stronger cues than they otherwise would, producing gender-stereotypical outcomes.

The strength of my research is that it examines practising managers anchored in their own institutional context. It compares the perceptions and attitudes of senior men and women who are at the same managerial level. Furthermore, rather than the more usual feminist approach which asks only women about management style, it sets the views of women alongside those of men. No previous British research has asked men their views about gendered management styles. Moreover, a defining feature of my research is that, rather than relying exclusively on standardized questionnaire data, I elicit respondents' own understandings of management style by means of open-ended questions and face-to-face interviewing. The survey data are complemented by substantial qualitative material based on interviews undertaken in the case study company known as 'Chip', a multinational computer firm described in the next chapter.

Let me begin by presenting my survey findings from typical questions about gender and leadership. Initially, I found that a high proportion of both women and men express the view that sex differences in management style *do* exist. On the whole they describe women's difference in positive terms. Asked generally about whether there are identifiable 'male' and 'female' styles of management, 69 per cent of women and 41 per cent of men think that there is a difference in style. It is interesting to note that a much higher proportion of women than men endorsed the view that there are sex differences in management style. Perhaps because women managers are in such a minority, they are more conscious of their difference from the men who predominate in management.

Typical descriptions by both men and women of the male style include: 'directive', 'self-centred/self-interested', 'decisive', 'aggressive', 'task oriented'. Adjectives used to describe the female style are: 'participative', 'collaborative', 'cooperative', 'coaching style', 'people oriented', 'caring'. Several women elaborated on this theme.

> The qualities that women bring to management tend not to be heavily control and power oriented, they tend to be more towards empowering people and getting the workers on board as opposed to telling them what to do ... I don't think many women feel comfortable with an authoritarian style.

> Women are generally more concerned to get a job done quickly and efficiently and are less concerned with pushing themselves forward and

making a mark in the organization. Men are more likely to look outside their department to play politics and ensure that they are noticed by the people that matter. Women prefer everybody to be as contented as possible whereas men are better able to put up with a hostile, aggressive atmosphere which is often a feature of business.

I think there are what I would call feminine and masculine characteristics that people have and I've experienced male managers who predominantly only portray what I call male characteristics – domineering, very task oriented, directive, impatient, those sort of things, and the more female characteristics I would describe as more encouraging, inclusive, mentoring type of way of managing somebody. Now in the past I would have said males tend to portray the male characteristics and women the female, though it's not exclusive. I see much more of the female characteristics being used by everybody nowadays and there are a few women I see who are using the male characteristics as well.

A number of men similarly describe differences in management style, identifying what they regarded as strengths in women's approach and decrying men's preoccupation with status and hierarchy.

Women have well-tuned antennae to the needs of other people, they have been brought up to deal with the needs of other people, almost above their own. So they are better managers of people . . . the female style is more sell – selling an idea they want you to do, whereas the male style is more tell – go and do it.

Males are status aware. Women are there to do a good job and be recognized and rewarded for that job, and they're actually not so bothered where they sit in the hierarchy. Men are very bothered about where they sit in the hierarchy and they're not necessarily so interested in the work, they're just more interested in the progress, because their status outside of the company is so much reflected in what they do. People ask you what job you do, how big's your budget, how big's your factory, is your factory bigger than my factory?

Women deal well with detail and I think a lot of low-quality work in business is done because people don't deal with things at the right level of the detail because of being overconfident, which is something I would criticize myself for doing.

The other set of oppositions respondents draw upon to describe sex differences in managerial style are those to do with reason versus emotion. Some men were particularly perceptive about the limitations of prevailing stereotypes and are concerned to emphasize that they do not fit the management style of women and men in their firm. These men see difference, but are inclined to reverse the standard terms by which women's difference is defined. For example,

> Inevitably women do tend to handle things from a slightly different tack . . . sort of rational . . . they tend to come at things from a much quieter perspective and particularly men can tend to go at things aggressively whereas women will argue their point more logically and retain their temper more consistently.

The views of the former head of human resources are interesting in this context because, although he appears to subscribe to the popular version of women's management style, he goes on to paint a more complex picture. He begins by saying that 'women's management style is coaching, enabling and nurturing rather than controlling and directing', and that this is the style of the future. He then proceeds to describe women first as rational and then as emotional, all the while deconstructing the standard dichotomy.

> Men and women are different in terms of the way they think and the way they act. Men are conditioned to be action oriented, what we call in Chip 'the ready-fire-aim syndrome'. So you get lots of smoke and clouds and dust and not a lot happens at the end of it. Whereas women have got a much more objective, rational approach; they are not so caught up in the emotion of 'let's make something happen'. They are actually able to be more rational and objective and logical towards the problem. Men are more often driven by power and status and ego needs.

Reflecting further on the question of sex differences, he acknowledges that men too are emotional but covertly so:

> I do find women more emotional than men *externally*, in the sense that they are more able to show their emotions than men. Does that mean they're more emotional than men? Don't know. I know lots of men who churn over internally all the bloody time and never let it show. So what is the definition of emotional?

By contrast, some women respondents thought that women managers take a more holistic approach, 'stepping back from the nitty gritty detail and seeing the whole thing and making linkages between apparently separate things, they have a more systematic view of the world. I experience this when I sit in a meeting.' The same interviewee attributes this female characteristic to 'the way women are brought up, they see their mothers doing a lot of things in parallel, and it's to do with men having single track minds and focusing on getting one thing done before they move on to the next.'

Other women took up this theme of women's ability to cope with multiple tasks.

> Women are better managers because they juggle with their life anyway. I mean women are naturally better at coping with multiple tasks than men because they have to. More and more women work now, therefore if they have arranged their home life such that they have to play the role of the wife/mother and worker then they have to juggle and women just seem to be more adept at it. I mean I think if you put a man, most men in a woman's situation, the situation I'm in, they would fail dismally after about a week. They just don't have this ability to juggle. And I think that makes us women better at managing because we have this ability to have three or four or five plates spinning at any one time and that's the norm.

In fact, although these respondents regard these qualities as feminine ones, they are more specifically connected with responsibility for childrearing. The last two quotes are from women who are themselves mothers, which is atypical of the sample in which less than a third of women managers are mothers. These women attach value to skills learnt in the home, reflecting what has been and continues to be an important thread in feminist strategies to improve women's position in the labour market. Equal value or 'comparable worth' legislation developed to deal with the fact that many women's skills are drawn on by employers but are not remunerated at the rate of men's equivalent skills.

Feminist theorizing about skill argues that a major reason that women have failed to achieve recognition of the skills required for their work is that skills are not technically but socially determined (see, for example, Cockburn 1985; Phillips and Taylor 1980; Wajcman 1991). That is, the categories for evaluating skill definitions are themselves gender biased. The very recognition of a job as skilled reflects competencies possessed by men, not women. Skilled status has been traditionally identified with masculinity and with work that women do *not* do, whereas women's skills have been defined as non-technical and hence undervalued.

A key reason for the undervaluing of women's skills is that some skills are regarded by employers as 'natural' female attributes rather than skills developed through training and experience. The household, the place in which these skills are often acquired, either transmitted by other women or developed in the course of childrearing, is not recognized as a valid training ground. In an innovative piece of Australian research on job evaluation schemes, Cox and Leonard take the notion of a skills audit and broaden it to include all those skills that women learn and practise in their unpaid work but that remain unacknowledged. Their project shows that in their household and community based work many women develop 'technical, management, finance, interpersonal and organizational expertise which is transferable into paid work situations' (1991: 5). From my own survey it is evident that many of the qualities that both men and women attribute to a feminine style are associated with mothering. Indeed, better managers are frequently now cast in the mould of mothers. Yet most women who *are* mothers are still absent from the ranks of senior management.

Saying It Soft, Doing It Hard: Management in Practice

When we examine how respondents to the survey describe *their own* management style, either as 'participative style, people-handling skills, developing subordinates' or as 'leading from the front, drive, decisively directing subordinates', we find no significant difference between the men's and women's responses. As many as 81 per cent of all respondents describe their management style as 'participative style, people-handling skills, developing subordinates'. Only 19 per cent describe themselves as 'leading from the front, drive, decisively directing subordinates'. Similarly, both men and women equally cite 'people management' as the most important skill required to do their jobs successfully.

These findings reveal the extent to which people characterize themselves in terms of dominant cultural values. Research shows that men and women tend to stereotype their own behaviour according to learned ideas of gender-appropriate behaviour, just as they stereotype the behaviour of other groups (Epstein 1988). An integral part of the identity of men and women is the perception that they possess, respectively, masculine and feminine qualities. So it is not surprising that women and men respondents subscribe to gender stereotypes of management styles. At the same time, respondents describe themselves in terms that accord with the prevailing orthodoxy of good management practice, now strongly associated with a consultative style and a high level of interpersonal skills. Subscribing to a people-centred approach happens to correspond with the current vogue for 'soft' human resources management (see, for example, Blyton and Turnbull 1992; Storey 1992).

What is ironic is that the participatory and cooperative leadership style with which the majority of both men and women identify also corresponds to current notions about a 'female management style'. If true, it would suggest that, rather than women having to become like men to be effective managers, men are already becoming more like women. Clearly the problem with these data is that they are based on self-identification. Other studies have highlighted the limitations of leaders' self-reports (see reviews by Ferrario 1994; Powell 1993). We might expect managers' self-perceptions in this study to be similarly biased. Unfortunately, little research has been conducted on subordinates' responses to their own managers, especially in business settings. It may well be that managers of both sexes who perceive themselves as having a participatory style may, in practice, use the command-and-control style.

Certainly the picture that emerges at the more detailed case-study level is more complicated than the survey evidence suggests. Perhaps in a survey people answer in terms of what they would like their organizations to be like rather than what they are really like. The rise of 'management speak' makes it much more difficult to conduct research in this area, because managers of large multinationals now tend to use the language of the human resource management model. Indeed, this language may even be used by senior management to mask the high degree of uncertainty and ambiguity that characterizes the current situation of many organizations.

When managers are asked to discuss more specifically their own work practices, a gap between beliefs and behaviour emerges. The evidence from my qualitative case-study material confirms that a major discrepancy exists between the rhetoric of 'soft' management and the 'hard' reality of practice. As Sisson argues, while the management 'rhetoric may be the people-centred approach of the "soft" version: the reality is the cost reduction approach of the "hard" version' (1994a: 15). Many of my interviewees commented that with the almost continuous 'downsizing' of companies, management is returning to a more traditional hierarchical structure. Macho management is again in the ascendancy. As the most senior woman manager in one company explained:

> The culture of the organization is becoming much more directive, much more controlled from head office ... flexibility, empowerment, those sort of values, are not high on people's priorities just at the moment because of the crisis the company is going through ... when things are tough people like to be in control and pull back control ... there's much more structure, much more rigidity. The word that is being used is discipline ... and these changes in management style favour a male style ... management say the right things on diversity issues but their actions are less clear. The actual tangible results are getting worse.

It is symptomatic of the business environment that she and several of the other senior women are leaving the company where they had initially prospered.

Male managers also expressed concern about the changes that were taking place. According to one respondent, 'we have returned to the 1960s military style of management by brutality, shouting louder, hit them harder and threaten them to death until they're frightened and they do what they're told.' He went on to contrast this with his preferred 'SAS or Israeli crack troops' style of leadership, which he described as 'working in very tight teams without massive hierarchies and lots of bullying. Simple pragmatism that says we are the best, this is our vision, and these are the goals we have to attain.'

The most pressing issue for managers at the time of my interviews was the problem of downsizing. Making people redundant was a frequent activity. Coping with uncertainty within the organization was also a constant theme. All my respondents found this process difficult and no obvious gender differences in managerial style emerged in how they accomplished the task. Likewise, when I asked people to talk about how they handled difficult and conflictual issues, no gender differences emerged. Rather both men and women related similar stories about dealing with such issues as pay, performance and retrenchment. As one female manager said:

> I hate having to make people redundant but I've been doing it for five years. I still don't find it any easier. But that's not true, I find I *can* detach myself more emotionally from it than I used to be able to. Nobody likes doing that. I'm used to giving feedback both good and negative and I do think it's important people know. I've had to sack people, so I've been through all that side too. I've had to deal with an alcoholic, I've had to deal with somebody moonlighting. I can't say it's very pleasant but I felt I had to deal with it. Why should they get away with it when all the other people are working hard?

A male told me that his worst experience as a manager had been reducing the income of a group he managed.

> I was a manager at the Aberdeen office at the time and the prices of houses were more expensive than London. So the guys got an Aberdeen allowance, which amounted to an extra 15 per cent of their salary. And then the company decided to remove that allowance, quite a huge percentage to lose. And I felt it was the hardest time for me because I was a manager in the company and therefore I had to carry out the company's wishes. The house prices had fallen, these guys had high mortgages and the company had taken away the support to help. So that was a difficult time – a bit emotional for me. I certainly fell out with my bosses at that time.

Managing had become extremely difficult in this fast-contracting company. Many managers had not received a substantial pay rise for years. Indeed, at the time of my interviews, the company had implemented a corporate-wide pay freeze throughout the UK. As a result good performance could not be rewarded adequately. The context made it hard to deal with subordinates who were not performing well. Several managers recounted stories around this theme. The first is from a woman attempting to discipline someone when retrenchment packages are ripe for the taking. She describes it as her 'worst management decision'.

> I inherited a guy and I felt that we should have fired him rather than making him redundant, but I could never quite tie him down. He never ever performed, but I couldn't prove it a hundred per cent. Somehow I could never quite get the goals to actually reflect whether it was his doing, or somebody else's, no matter how much I tried. Basically the guy walked out with a large sum of money when he didn't really deserve it. He should have been on disciplinary. I didn't manage that too well and what really upset me was he wrote to me thanking me for the large cheque I'd just given him.

The next two stories typically illustrate the harsh environment in which managers are now operating. The first account is from a woman manager and the second from a man.

> I do have a situation where a particular person is supposed to do quite a lot of marketing communications work for me. Two or three times there's been bad delivery of the work and I had to sort it. But I don't have time to do that now, and to go on and on suggesting training courses, books to read – some people just do not want to learn. It's got

very hard now. If all the work gets outsourced then he will be made redundant.

There's less people management time available now. Motivation levels have changed over the last few years. People aren't getting rewarded the same as they used to in terms of salary, and there's less time available to spend with them on things that bother them. They work longer hours which affects their home life, there's less flexibility to do the things they might have done. You're having to screw down on what their core role is and cut down on what's good to do, nice to do, in order to concentrate on what they're really here for.

Finally, I recount at length how a male manager describes following the routine set of mediating procedures that the company has in place for dealing with questions of performance. Fair and proper procedures are time-consuming, and he too ends his account by acknowledging that his managerial style has hardened because of the current situation.

I had an individual here who was working hard but not actually doing the job that I wanted him to do. We had a meeting and went through the plan and direction, and what he felt he should be doing. There was a clear mismatch. The outcome of that meeting was that we both decided to think about it for another day or so and then get back to the round table and come up with reasons why we felt so strongly. When we met again I was able to present more evidence of what I thought he should be doing, and why. He wasn't and it was the same after the next meeting, which ended with me just saying, 'well, I'm sorry, that's the way it is and you're just going to have to accept it or find yourself another job.' Now he was annoyed at the time but since then he's come around to my way of thinking and he's actually doing the job that I wanted him to do and that worked very well. But it took quite a lot of time and quite a lot of effort and I'm not sure if that situation happened again that I would actually do the same thing. I think it was the right thing to do. I think I'd be more inclined *these days* to turn around and say, 'that's the way it is.' It's bad news, but that's the reality.

The business context of continuous restructuring and job losses has greatly intensified pressures for senior managers. Insecurity about the future is pervasive. The traditional career-for-life model, based on employment security and promotion prospects, has been replaced by a climate of fear and anxiety about the very real prospect of redundancy in many organizations. These conditions are not conducive to sustaining work relationships based on high levels of trust and

cooperation. Rather, the logic of survival results in heightened individualistic competition for a dwindling number of career opportunities. In this economic climate, both men and women feel the need
to conform to the male stereotype of management because it is still,
in practice, the only one regarded as effective.

This situation was summed up neatly in the words of a male
respondent who clearly felt so constrained:

> In any organization there is a norm for success and everyone has to
> conform to that. In some organizations that norm is very male, white
> macho in style; women are expected to adhere to that norm. I am not
> saying that it is the only norm in Chip, but the white, Western, male
> macho culture is ingrained . . . Macho means not being willing to look
> at yourself, being closed to certain things, being certain about every-
> thing in life. Attitudes such as: I cannot possibly allow my defences to
> come down; it's impossible to talk to anyone honestly about how I feel.
> And never allowing people to see me cry.

You Can't Take the 'Man' out of Management

There are thus powerful organizational imperatives that dictate management style and goals and permit few substantial modifications in
management approach. This point is particularly important in relation to Rosener's argument discussed at the outset of this chapter.
Her survey is based on managers in medium-size, non-traditional
organizations in which, significantly, women have come to management via unconventional career paths. My research is based on five
male-dominated multinational corporations whose organizational
structure and institutional politics are very different. Furthermore,
the vast majority of managers have had conventional internal career
paths in these companies. Respondents have moved around within
the company. Over 80 per cent of both men and women were
recruited to their present post through internal promotion. So both
groups have had equal exposure to the promotion system in their
company.

In sharp contrast to Rosener's sample, selection processes and
organizational socialization have fundamentally shaped the management approach of both women and men managers in my study.
Senior managers of either sex, who hold positions with equivalent
status and power in their companies, behave in broadly similar ways.
Whether a diversity of management styles is accepted and successful

in less conventional organizations, or at lower levels of management, remains an open question.

Given these constraints, it should come as no surprise that many women managers adapt and survive by being more male than the men. The statement of one man in my survey is typical:

> In general female managers prefer a participative, consensual style of management but at *senior* level in my experience there is a 'Thatcher factor' – a tendency to be more stereotypically male than typical male managers. That is, decisive, even aggressive, and avoiding any interacting except in formal professional contexts often associated with 'I never needed equal opportunities to get where I did so why do they?' approach.

This comment partly reflects the 'iron maiden' stereotype of strong women working in male-dominated organizations who do not conform to the more usual feminine roles, so well described by Kanter. However, as Kanter argues, it also reflects a strategy adopted by some women in order to succeed: 'some women try to stay away from the role traps by bending over backwards not to exhibit any characteristics that would reinforce female stereotypes. This strategy, too, is an uneasy one, for it takes continual watchful effort, and it may involve unnatural self-distortion' (1977: 237).

Although I have been emphasizing the ways in which the symbolic representation of management is sharply gendered as male, it is precisely because there is substance to these stereotypes that they continue to have such enduring force. In general, women and men tend to conform in practice to their gender roles. Women who deviate by adopting the male role pay a heavy price. Even if there are no consistent gender differences in management style, there are certainly profound gender differences in experience, as we see in subsequent chapters.

The crucial point to be borne in mind is that the strength of the ideology of sex difference is precisely its capacity to be flexible. To say that management is identified as male does not imply that there is a single uniform idea of what good management is. Indeed, participatory involvement was seen as the key characteristic of management during the Human Relations movement of the 1930s and 1940s. Even so, this precursor of the current fashion for 'transformational management' was entirely identified as a male leadership style. Ideas of what constitutes effective management will necessarily change over time. The point is that the qualities associated with effective management are not gender neutral. While current debates reflect a blurring of the familiar set of oppositions in which hard management is male and soft management is female, it is still men who are best placed to lay claim to whatever characteristics are seen to be the desirable ones.

It is important not to confuse the issue of valuing 'feminine' qualities in management with the issue of including more women in senior positions. The revaluing of the female style and a stress on diversity rather than equality will not necessarily improve women's prospects of success. Instead of producing an influx of women into senior management, it is just as likely that men will appropriate this rediscovered 'feminine' style and add it to their traditionally male repertoire.. Indeed it could be said that performing a 'feminine' style has a completely different meaning for men than for women. For men this style is not naturalized as part of the self, and is therefore rewarded and can be mobilized as an occupational resource. Whereas men will be advantaged by adding new qualities to those they are already deemed to have, women will continue to be seen as offering feminine qualities only.

The danger is that by focusing on women's individual characteristics rather than the structural barriers they face, the recent managerial discourse about gendered management styles may mask the extent to which women are losing out in the current business climate. It is naive to believe that the revaluing of women's 'difference' will succeed where 'equal' opportunities have failed. A stress on women's difference leaves untouched the mythical male figure of the rational, instrumental manager. It therefore slides easily into a reinforcement of traditional sex stereotypes of managers and may even contribute to new regimes of gender hierarchy within organizations. Whichever way women play it, we will never make the grade as men.

4

The Corporate Career: 'Why Can't a Woman be More Like a Man?'

Careers have traditionally provided a set of organizing principles around which managers in large-scale organizations have been able to structure both their professional and private lives. The 'psychological contract' between employer and employee has been based upon loyalty and commitment to the organization in exchange for the incremental increases in authority, status and financial remuneration associated with a corporate career (Rousseau 1995). The combined promises of job security and personal advancement within corporate hierarchies have constituted the major rewards of the twentieth-century middle-class career.

Since the 1980s two fundamental changes to the nature of the corporate career have received a great deal of attention from academic observers. The immense transformations in industrial organization and technological change that have resulted from increasing global competitive pressures mean that organizations and careers within them are becoming increasingly precarious. The other issue is the changed role of women and the extent to which 'organization man' (Whyte 1957) has been joined by 'organization woman'. Although historically men's careers were built on women's exclusion, women have now succeeded in entering management and the professions in significant numbers. Does this mean that there is an increasing convergence between male and female career paths?

In this chapter I investigate gendered aspects of the career in a post-equal opportunities world. The research explores the interaction between formal equal opportunity in employment policies and the extent to which organizational processes, particularly in a context of corporate restructuring, continue to obstruct women's career advancement. In this chapter I argue that the notion of a career is a highly problematic and gendered concept. We will see that the few women who have made it into senior positions are in most respects indistinguishable from men in equivalent positions. However, accommodating to the male model is not enough to guarantee women success. Despite their own efforts, their career progression is ultimately blocked. Women's experience of management suggests it is still men who have the power to define what constitutes the occupation, and men who dominate it.

Gendered Careers

Before I consider gender differences in careers, it is worth outlining the basic characteristics of the typical organizational career of the 1950s and 1960s. Traditionally, the managerial career has consisted of a series of related jobs through which a person moved in a sequential manner. The term 'career' designated occupations located within organizations expressed in terms of hierarchical, bureaucratic career structures. The notion of progress within an organization meant regular successive stages of development with increasing responsibility and more highly paid posts. The criteria for advancement were normally associated with length of service, ability and performance. Personal success tended to be closely related to various age-related stages, with careers being consolidated in middle-age. An internal labour market could deliver a lifelong career in a single organization. 'Organization men' identified with and were deeply loyal to the organization in which their career was made. Other aspects of life, such as the family, were subordinated to the demands of the firm.

Over the last two decades the bureaucratic career structures enjoyed by a large proportion of managerial and professional staff have been destabilized. A common feature of the organizational restructuring in this period has been the attempt to move to 'flexible', 'flatter' and 'leaner' corporate structures. Fewer of those in middle-class occupations are now guaranteed long-term career advancement. In many organizations the current situation is characterized by a high degree of economic insecurity, with increasing risks of redundancy. Increasingly managers are encouraged to 'manage their own careers' and to contemplate moves between organizations as well as moves between employment and self-employment (Handy 1994; Brown and Scase 1994). They may thus be forced to pursue 'flexible' rather than 'bureaucratic' careers. As a result of these developments, Scase and Goffee (1993) have suggested that managers may cease to be psychologically immersed in their work roles and become less committed to career success as it has been conventionally understood (Heckscher 1995; Newell and Dopson 1996). However, we shall see that the senior managers in my survey largely fit the traditional model of the organizational career. So I would caution against the more exaggerated claims made by management gurus about the demise of the bureaucratic paradigm.

During the 1980s the issue of gender differences in careers came to prominence. At the same time the underrepresentation or marginal status of women in senior management became a subject of debate. The term 'glass ceiling' was coined in the mid-1980s (*Wall Street Journal*, 24 March 1986) to denote a set of invisible barriers obstructing women's promotion opportunities in management and impeding the upward mobility of women beyond the middle levels. After some years of the implementation of equal opportunity policies, there is now increasing recognition of the informal barriers that inadvertently reproduce a world in which there are so few senior women managers. As feminists have argued for a long time, although discriminatory employment policies have become more difficult to maintain, a formal equality of access is not adequate to achieve a real equality of practice (Cockburn 1991). Indeed the post-equal opportunity workplace may be generating new forms of organizational exclusion as well as maintaining old forms.

It is increasingly acknowledged that the very concept of a managerial career, with its hierarchical model of continuous service and regular promotion progress, is gendered (Dex 1987; Beechey 1987; Evetts 1996). Women's life-cycle patterns of work and childbearing have not equipped them for a career in management. The career stage when the workload and commitment necessary to succeed are most intensive coincides with peak childrearing years. The developmental trajectory of a career that fits the life course of men is directly at odds with the family life-cycle. Women's careers, which are generally 'broken' or 'interrupted' in order to have and to care for children, are thereby rendered not just different but deficient.

In the face of these structural barriers, many women have adopted an alternative strategy for their careers. Crompton and Sanderson (1990) distinguish between linear organizational careers, which involve promotion to positions of managerial responsibility, and practitioner/occupational careers, which involve doing the job but might include taking breaks and part-time employment. The practitioner option has offered professional women a way of combining family and career. In her study of careers among a group of scientists and engineers, Evetts (1996) employs a similar notion of 'career accommodation' to describe the women in her study, most of whom opted out of career promotion for a period to have a family. In the US, the 'mommy track' describes a variety of organizational arrangements that allow women in management the opportunity to spend more time at home with their young children (Schwartz 1992). Although part of the career strategy of many women involves such breaks from their paid work, as Evetts notes, activities other than paid work do not contribute positively to their promotion prospects. Indeed, they damage them.

Personal and family responsibilities enter linear career structures only as a way of explaining the lack of promotion achievement of some career builders. As a result, equal opportunity policies have been largely preoccupied with enabling women to combine family responsibilities with a career, because this dual responsibility is seen as the main block to their career advancement. Indeed, there is a widespread perception that it is now much easier than it was to manage this conflict. But the empirical evidence for this optimism is equivocal to say the least, as I will show. In practice, 'family friendly' policies are mainly available to women at the higher end of the occupational hierarchy. However, even at this level, few women are taking them up. The point is illustrated by a comment from the director of personnel at my case study company. When asked how many senior people take advantage of their excellent equality policies, he said that actually no one did. After further questioning, he admitted that to do so would adversely affect how the company viewed them. They would be seen as less committed to their jobs and therefore less suitable management material. Equality policies have by no means displaced the male model of management.

Marriage and fatherhood have not presented serious career dilemmas for men seeking promotion in professional and managerial occupations. In their study of sex discrimination in employment, Collinson et al. provide extensive evidence of the way employers' preconceptions about gender roles in the family affect decision-making. 'For men, real, imagined or potential domestic responsibilities were usually evaluated as a positive indication of stability, flexibility, compatibility and motivation, while for women, they were often viewed negatively as confirmation of unreliability and a short-term investment in work' (1990: 193–4). This discrepancy is not a matter of favouring men over women in all circumstances, but simply reflects the perception of jobs themselves as gendered. Indeed, employers positively discriminate in selecting women 'homemakers' for jobs linked with low pay and low status in female-dominated workforces (Curran 1988). But where a job such as that of a manager is sex-typed for men, the 'ideal candidate' is a family man.

The approach in much of the literature on gender and careers tends to focus on women's difference: the way women experience different careers as a result of their family circumstances. In my study, however, the women have adapted to the predominant male model of a successful manager and are pursuing the same organizational careers as the men. They have made a conscious choice either not to have children or to organize childcare and domestic life so as to be able to dedicate themselves to their careers. Yet they are still treated as different from men and their career progress is blocked. The sexual contract thus constitutes *all* women as workers with domestic responsibilities.

Much recent feminist work, reviewed in chapter 2, has shifted its focus from the barriers faced by women in achieving equality within organizations to an emphasis on the way in which gender differences are actively constructed within organizations. These theories, particularly in relation to questions of organizational culture, have been elaborated with very little empirical foundation. Furthermore, much of the existing research suffers from treating women managers in isolation from men. Failure to examine the experience of men within the same organization inevitably limits our understanding of how managers are made. This study aims to correct the imbalance by presenting comparative material on the attitudes and experiences of women and men managers. The particular concern here is to examine the role that gender plays in the construction of the managerial career.

Commitment to Work

The conventional view that, as workers, women are different from men has been used to argue that women are unsuitable for responsible positions, and as an explanation of their rarity in senior management. Major sex differences are said to exist in the hours that managers work and in their motivation towards paid employment. For example, Davidson and Cooper (1992: 16) and Scase and Goffee (1993: 85) both argue that women managers are more likely than men to be *job* rather than *career* oriented, concerned with the intrinsic rewards of the task at hand rather than with future career benefits. On their account, women are less instrumental, less interested in career advancement, and generally less committed to work.

However, as Guest (1992) notes, the concept of commitment is complex and difficult to define. Various measures have been used to evaluate the claim that women are less committed to work than men. Because it is actually very difficult to measure the quality or productivity of managerial work, commitment to work is often measured in terms of time spent at the workplace, the implication being that women are less committed to work because they work shorter hours than men (Powell 1993). Gender differences arise from the contrasting domestic circumstances of men and women managers and result in the more frequent experience of career disappointment among women.

Recent years have witnessed growing discussion of the intensification of work pressures on managers and a significant lengthening of their working week. For example, Scase and Goffee (1993) reported that most of the managers in their study worked an average week in excess of 50 hours (and were generally working harder than ever before). Similarly, a survey of British National Health Service top managers found that their average was 56 working hours per week (British NHS Women's Unit 1994). The question arises whether these long hours act as a disincentive to persons in middle management seeking promotion, particularly women. Not only is this issue of hours central to human capital theorists' explanations of women's unequal position. It is also at the heart of the current conceptions of the 'macho' manager, or the idea that being a manager requires total commitment and sacrifice to the organization. The job comes first, above all else. So it is important to consider at least two aspects of commitment: (attitudes to) hours of work, and what motivates people in their job settings.

An important first step is to establish the domestic position of the survey participants. The data confirm that in relation to family structures and the domestic division of labour the contrast between the situation of men and women is stark. As figure 4.1 shows, the marital status of the men and women managers is very different: 93 per cent of male managers are married or living with a partner as compared with 73 per cent of their female colleagues. Women managers are much more likely to be single, divorced or separated: 27 per cent against 7 per cent of men. Over two-thirds of the women managers surveyed do not have children, while over two-thirds of the men do have children living with them. However, the data show that by and large the men do not take primary responsibility for the care of their children. Of respondents with children, 94 per cent of women, compared to only 15 per cent of men, report that they have primary responsibility for their children. As a consequence, the average weekly hours of housework (defined as cooking, cleaning, laundry, shopping and childcare) for the women in the survey is 19 hours, whereas the average weekly total for men is 10 hours. This finding reinforces those of previous studies, that even in dual-career households women are likely to shoulder more domestic work and childcare than their partners (see, for example, Hochschild 1990).

Given these striking differences in household type and in the distribution of housework, it is remarkable that we do not find markedly different attitudes to work and hours of work by sex. Over 60 per cent of female and male respondents report that they work an average week in excess of 50 hours, with over 16 per cent of both men and women working over 60 hours. When asked 'how many nights a month do you spend away from home on business?' the replies are as follows: 8 per cent of men and 18 per cent of women spend no nights away; of those who spend some nights away, 74 per cent of men and 66 per cent of women spend 1–4 nights; 12 per cent of men and 13 per cent of women spend 5–8 nights; and 6 per cent of men and 4 per cent of women spend 9 or more. Even when asked about changing their

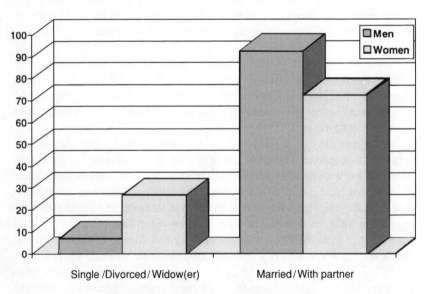

Figure 4.1   Marital status of managers

hours of work, no differences emerge. Of those (64%) who express a desire for change in their working hours, over two-thirds of both men and women would prefer to work shorter hours and one-third say they would like different hours. The NHS survey referred to earlier also found no significant gender differences in hours worked. The finding of no significant difference in the hours men and women work is contrary to the common perception that men work longer hours than women. The need to work long hours should not therefore act as a barrier to women's promotion. However, *perceptions* about women's ability and willingness to work long hours differ from the reality and continue to influence women's promotion paths negatively.

As to the issue of work motivation, I drew on a variety of sources for the survey questions. Some derive from material successfully exploited by Storey et al. (1997) in their comparative research on British and Japanese managerial careers. Other questions are similar to those used by Scase and Goffee (1993). From the data presented here (table 4.1), it is evident that there are in fact few sex differences in overall responses to questions about motivation to work. Interestingly, the main sources of motivation for both men and women are intrinsic to the work itself, that is, a sense of achievement and enjoying the job. In a large-scale survey of American managers, Jacobs (1992) also found broad similarities in the attributes of jobs favoured by men and women, both ranking 'meaningful work' first. Likewise, Grant and Porter's study (1994) demonstrates an extremely high level of commitment to occupation among women managers. The authors mount a strong case for the centrality of work in the formation of these women's identity.

Close inspection of these results reveals two small but statistically significant differences between men and women. Women appear to enjoy power more than men and they are slightly less concerned about financial reward. The latter difference suggests that women are less instrumentally motivated but it is much smaller than the sociological literature would suggest. This unexpected finding may be explained by the high proportion of men in the survey who financially support full-time housewives. Very few of the women are financially supporting their partners. However, it might also be an adaptation by women to limited career opportunities. Similarly, women may enjoy power more because they are generally less accustomed to it, or have had to succeed against greater odds to achieve it. Indeed, women may attach more significance to the exercise of power precisely to compensate for reduced financial rewards. Overall, however, this research finds little evidence for the traditional assumption that

Table 4.1   Percentage of respondents mentioning each source of motivation

		Very important	Fairly important	Not very important	Not at all important
Prospect of	Men	24	51	22	3
promotion	Women	20	52	26	3
Financial	Men	35	55	8	2
reward	Women	24	56	19	–
Status	Men	6	59	32	3
	Women	16	44	34	6
Sense of	Men	85	15	–	1
achievement	Women	88	10	–	2
Fear of	Men	14	33	41	12
failure	Women	17	37	26	20
Contributing	Men	44	48	7	1
to company	Women	45	47	9	–
Enjoying the	Men	73	24	3	–
job	Women	86	14	–	1
Meeting	Men	44	49	6	1
targets	Women	47	44	8	2
Respect from	Men	48	44	8	–
colleagues	Women	55	42	3	–
Developing	Men	36	54	9	1
people	Women	37	55	8	–
Enjoying	Men	13	40	40	7
power	Women	21	48	22	10

women's motivation to work is radically different from men's. The very different domestic situations of men and women managers do not result in sharply sex-differentiated attachment to work, let alone the hours these managers actually do work.

Career Progression and Barrier Methods

Women's lack of promotion into senior management cannot then simply be understood in terms of either their individual characteristics or their family situation. Indeed most women have had to forgo having children in favour of their careers. I now discuss other factors within the workplace that may act as barriers to career progression.

It is important to remember the organizational context. As already indicated, the companies in the study were chosen because of their exemplary equal opportunities policies. The companies are all flagship members of 'Opportunity 2000'. They all have explicit and highly visible policies to increase the number of women at all levels of their organizations, although in fact the main focus is on the progress of women in management. Common initiatives include flexible work arrangements, the provision of some kind of childcare or career break option, generous maternity leave provisions, and close scrutiny of recruitment and promotion practices. Some of the companies also have a women's network, provide women-only training courses and have policies against sexual harassment.

These equality provisions fit within the broader framework of human resource management policies. As I argued in chapter 1, they are regarded as just one facet of corporate systems for maximizing human potential within the workforce. In general, these companies would see themselves as operating the textbook model of 'soft' human resource management (Sisson 1994a). This approach is essentially people centred, emphasizing communication, motivation and leadership. The personnel managers responsible for the implementation of these policies all spoke about the need to promote profound cultural change and to raise consciousness about equality issues through such initiatives as intensive workshops. In sum, these are companies who profess a serious commitment to equal opportunities at the very highest levels of decision-making in the organization.

A number of questions in the survey address the theme of career progression. It is at this point that marked sex differences begin to emerge. Men and women express very different views of women's prospects within their organization. Whereas 70 per cent of men think that men and women have equal chances of promotion in their company, fewer than 40 per cent of the women think the same. In fact, nearly three-quarters (71%) of women believe that a 'glass ceiling' limits women's ability to move up the ladder, a view shared by almost a third of the men. This finding raises doubts about the practical success of equal opportunity policies in these companies.

Nearly twice as many women as men report they have experienced barriers in their career. When asked to nominate up to three principal barriers encountered, over a third (34%) of the men but only 18 per cent of the women say they have not experienced any barriers. Among those who have experienced barriers, the four most commonly cited by men and women alike are that senior management is perceived to be a 'club', the prejudice of colleagues, the lack of career guidance, and family commitments (see table 4.2). It is perhaps surprising that in companies with such developed human resource policies the lack of career guidance is perceived to be a major barrier for both sexes.

However, there are substantial differences in the kinds of barriers that women and men typically experience. Significantly more women than men regard the prejudice of colleagues and the 'clubbiness' of senior management as obstacles to their progress. It is striking that 76 per cent of women as against 43 per cent of men cite senior management as a 'club' or the prejudice of colleagues as a barrier. This finding accords with Coe's (1992) research, that the greatest barrier encountered by senior women managers in their career is the men's 'club'. The most recent British Institute of Management survey of its members, which replicates Coe's study, confirms that 'the Old Boys network remains the most significant single barrier for women' (Charlesworth 1997: 33).

Furthermore, there is a marked difference between men and women in their reports of sexual discrimination/harassment as a barrier to their career development, with one in six women saying

Table 4.2 Percentage of respondents mentioning principal barriers in their career

	Men	Women
Inflexible working patterns	6	14
Family commitments[a]	44	43
Lack of adequate childcare	3	8
Lack of career guidance	45	50
Lack of training provision	9	5
Prejudice of colleagues	11	23
Lack of personal motivation/confidence	19	21
Senior management seen as a 'club'	32	54
Social pressures	1	10
Sexual discrimination/harassment	1	17
Insufficient education	11	13

[a] Here the data refer only to respondents with children.

they experienced this barrier compared to only one in a hundred men. In a separate question asking respondents if they had ever experienced any form of discrimination at work, just over half of the women say they have experienced sexual discrimination. A slightly higher proportion of women with children (59%) report they experienced sexual discrimination. In this context, it is interesting to note that when it comes to listing sources of positive support in their careers, three times as many women (22%) as men mention the importance of a female boss or female role model.

How is it that systematic barriers to women's advancement into senior positions still operate in companies with such model equal opportunity policies? While it has been relatively easy for women to gain employment at the lower levels of these organizations, it is much more difficult for them to reach middle and senior executive positions. In all the companies surveyed there is a clearly identifiable level past which even the few senior women do not advance, but the causes are not obvious. There is truly a 'glass ceiling'. There is a great divergence between espoused company policy to eliminate discrimination on the grounds of sex and organizational reality. The lack of significant sex differences in respondents' overall attitudes and managerial style is striking when compared to the pronounced sex differences in perceptions of career barriers.

In order to explore these issues I present qualitative material drawn from my interviews with managers in the case study company. What emerges is the salience of informal institutionalized practices which continue to operate despite considerable changes in the formal norms of these companies. The construction of the managerial job as male is especially strong at the most senior levels. Research shows that adopting procedures that are apparently fair does not guarantee fair outcomes. Strict adherence to suitability criteria can still lead to the continued appointment of white men (Webb and Liff 1988; Rubin 1997). These criteria, as we shall see, are themselves tainted by gender bias.

Accounting for the Careers of the Men and Women in the Study

Before examining the experience of managers at the case study company, it is important to describe the kind of company involved. This description provides a context for understanding the ways in which the organization and its culture have changed.

The company is a computer firm which is referred to as 'Chip'. Its headquarters in the UK are located in a greenfield site, within commuting distance from London. The purpose-built structure resembles a large airport hangar – an enormous, fully enclosed modernist space with tight security on entry. Once inside, people can spend their working day entirely within this space. There is an internal corridor, known as The Street, which has shops, a bank, a chemist and cafés along its length. Apart from a few upstairs offices for directors, the work space is open plan with work stations partitioned off from one another. Chip operates a 'hot desk' system, so that on arrival people are simply allocated a work site for the day. Employees have a locker in which to keep a few private things. This working arrangement was disconcerting for the researcher, an industrial sociologist trained to pick up cues about people from their office surroundings! In this company, each time I arrived the interviewee had been allocated an office at random for the interview.

Chip expanded at a phenomenal pace during the 1970s and 1980s. It is a company that prides itself on being at the cutting edge of corporate strategies and employment practices. For example, Chip boasted an exceptionally large training and development budget, with both women and men attending courses up to 15 days a year. The company was innovative in its products and in its organizational style. The latest fashions in human resource management were taken up with enthusiasm. Everyone had high expectations of career progression within the company.

A clearly structured career path to management existed, the most common being for men with an engineering background to move from jobs as field service engineers up through various levels of the hierarchy. Fewer women had followed this traditional route. It was more common for women to have a degree in computer science or to have joined Chip as computer programmers, entry points that provided no standard route to senior management jobs. However, some women had risen to senior management from routine secretarial/administrator levels.

As a company, Chip is deeply committed to equality policies. These policies have a high profile both externally and internally. The company provides a crèche facility, flexible working hours, model policies on parental leave and career breaks, and an active women's network. It is one of the initial group of companies that signed up for the Opportunity 2000 campaign in 1991. At the same time it appointed a senior manager to oversee equal opportunity policy and published an ambitious goal to 'employ women at all levels in the company in the same proportion to the total number of women in the Chip workforce'. Indeed, being an American-owned multinational, the discourse of equality and diversity reverberates in a more obvious way at Chip than in most British companies. I was told of mornings when an image of the managing director of the US corporate head-quarters would be beamed on to the computer screens to speak directly to the UK workforce, often stressing the importance of diversity policies for company success. As a new fast-growing high-tech company with an open, meritocratic organizational philosophy and leading edge policies, Chip offers an ideal case study.

Interviewees speak of the early days in Chip with great affection and loyalty.

> High growth. High opportunities for people. It was the norm to change your job every year. If you didn't, you wondered why you were stagnating. Massive opportunities if you wanted to grasp them. (female)

> There was no need for a union. People gave their all to Chip. There was an informal promise of lifetime employment . . . It was a very open, consensual culture. Meetings were like gestalt groups – people talking very openly. Leaving Chip was like leaving a long marriage! (male)

> Originally there were some very strong company values about integrity, doing the right thing. And doing the best thing for Chip. So the sorts of qualities we were looking for in individuals were integrity, commitment and obviously ability in the role that they were doing. When I first joined Chip, it wasn't like the other companies I had worked for – it was something very different. There was certainly a culture of achievement and success and enthusiasm. (male)

It is striking that women, as well as men, felt the same intense identification with the company.

> Chip was an amazing company to work for. It was unstructured, there was no formal route for getting anything done. It was very much about who you knew and people were totally cooperative. I came from a merchant bank which was absolutely the opposite – very formal, very structured, very hierarchical, you called your boss Mr so and so. In Chip everybody called everybody by the Christian name from the chief exec down and there are no private parking spaces, everybody uses the same restaurant. I absolutely loved it . . . if you cut me through the middle I would have been Chip through and through. (female)

The equal opportunities officer describes Chip's most successful equality policy as not a policy at all but rather as an expression of the company culture that prevailed during the period of massive expansion, when everybody could fulfil their potential. It was during this phase that a number of secretaries had risen from a secretarial level to middle management, and a few even to senior management. The female head of personnel recounts that:

> Chip in its earlier years, with its absolute need for talent, was a Mecca for women who had any kind of skills and ability because there weren't enough people to go round and there was more work to do and if anybody had a bright idea they were allowed to go and explore it, so you'd draw in the people who could help you and if there was somebody sitting there who demonstrated some ability, well they'd be the first to be drawn in. It's not a very classist environment, at least it wasn't, it's gotten much more hierarchical of late but it started out as very eclectic, you know everybody was in the team and therefore in the UK or in the US or almost in any country when you went into Chip you felt that sense of opportunity. It had 35 per cent growth rate a year.

One woman describes her career development in just this vein:

> I came to Chip originally for interview for a secretary. About two or three months later they rang me back and said, are you interested in coming to join us as an administrator, and I said yes please. Not having a clue what an administrator was. I got the job and I joined a very small branch and the atmosphere was just tremendous. It was so good because there were only two of us, the other lady was very senior and had been around for a long while. I jumped up a few steps on that ladder basically because I was just not bound by anything. Because this was all new to me I hadn't been told it's impossible. I got close to some of the sales guys and got them to let me have some of their work. So all the way there were no doors shut, it seemed wherever you pushed it was OK to go and do it ... At that time we were running a sales trainee programme and I have to be very honest. I didn't actually take an awful lot of thought about whether I should go for it or not. I just knew that I'd worked with some of these salesmen, they weren't any more intelligent than I was, and I knew that with a little bit of training I could do exactly what they did every day. So I went, I applied for the sales trainee programme. I was the only woman. Six months through the training and out into sales and then really just on up through a couple of junior ranks of sales and virtually every year just achieved and moved on up. I now manage a sales group.

It would be easy to assume that a company described in these terms would have an unusually high number of senior women managers. However, this is not the case, despite the positive efforts to improve equal opportunity policies within the company. Just under one-third of the Chip workforce are women, and analysis of the demographic data reveals very little change in the position of women at managerial levels, particularly the most senior. Although nearly 14 per cent of managerial and professional positions are held by women, women form only about 5 per cent of senior management.

There is also some evidence that women are not being rewarded in accordance with their assessed performance. Salary increases are based on performance and, as other studies on gender and performance pay show (Kessler 1994), there is a significant disparity in the rewards received by men and women at Chip. Yet there is little general awareness of this disparity being systematic gender discrimination. In fact several women who were being paid less than their male counterparts account for the gap in particularistic terms. An explanation of these gender differences must be sought elsewhere, by examining in detail the promotion systems operating at Chip.

'Getting On': Formal Policy and Informal Practices

Chip has a very progressive organizational model of recruitment and selection. Once a vacancy is identified by a particular department, management notifies Human Resources, who then 'open job post' the vacancy on an internal computer system accessible to all employees. Company policy is that all jobs must be posted internally before vacancies can be advertised in the external labour market. The vacancies advertised on screen are generally in the form of fairly comprehensive job descriptions detailing skills and knowledge required, together with experience and key behaviours necessary to perform the job. All applications are then screened by the recruiting manager, and the final selection is made only after interviewing candidates. This model represents an ordered, logical sequence of events in which employment decisions are made in relation to the formal requirements of the job and the abilities of workers. This systematic process is designed to eliminate bias and subjectivity and to lead to fair, meritocratic decisions based on the suitability of candidates in terms of specified job-related criteria.

The findings from my research suggest that internalization of the organizational model of selection is patchy at best, and that it operates most effectively at the lower levels of the company. As the director of personnel explains: 'In reality, open job posting is not so open because the individual manager is the person who makes the

selection, and the individual manager does it against the precon-
ceived model he has, in his head, for what a good manager is . . . we
can't take the subjectivity out of it.'

It is evident that the majority of departments use the methodology
in a superficial way, often in the process of rationalizing their decisions after the event. However, the criteria of suitability and acceptability remain crucial elements of the selection process, with
behavioural and social skills being judged by individual recruiting
managers. This finding tallies with other research on employers' extensive use of informal and implicit criteria of acceptability in selection procedures (Jenkins 1986; Curran 1988; Collinson et al. 1990).

Especially at the senior levels of the organization, many jobs are
filled without recourse to these formal procedures. At this level, a
more informal type of succession planning operates, using informal
networks to identify those people considered suitable. These candidates are selected on the basis of their track record in the organization and their visibility to their superiors.

Indeed, the most crucial factor for career success cited by interviewees is visibility, followed by the related factors of networks and
acceptability. As Collins has argued:

> The overriding fact is that an organizational career is made in a political
> environment, and success goes to those individuals who recognize that
> fact and act on it most assiduously. The one who makes it to the top is
> the organizational politician, concerned above all with informal ties,
> manoeuvering toward the crucial gate-keepers, avoiding the organiza-
> tional contingencies that trap the less wary. (1979: 31)

Visibility and networking go hand in hand, because it is essential to
be 'seen' to be doing your job well:

> It's the people who speak up in meetings, who make good points, who
> get themselves visible . . . men have been trained, conditioned that in
> order to get up the social hierarchy this is what you have to do, you have
> to take every opportunity to make yourself visible. Men make sure that
> everybody knows what a good job they've done. (male)

> There's no formal appraisal system because Chip works very much on
> a network of who you know, there can be barriers because you're not
> perhaps in the right place at the right time and know the right people.
> When opportunities come up, for example the current role that I'm
> in I knew that the guy was going to be moving on somewhere else
> and because I knew that I was able to pursue that opportunity . . . the
> barrier is the amount of time you've got for networking. (male)

I started to feel that success wasn't about how well you did, but about how much time you were spending telling everybody how well you were doing. I have to be honest with you. I dictated a travel justification this morning to my secretary ... and the last three sentences were nothing to do with the justification. They were about telling people how brilliant it was to get this piece of work, and I think I am going to start doing this more often than I used to. (male)

Many men speak about the pervasive power of the old boy network or men's club and its subtle mode of operation. At its core is a group of men with a shared background, who have worked with each other over many years and meet socially at conferences and in local pubs. Since the recession has hit hard, there are now fewer opportunities to meet outside the workplace but it appears that this has in no way weakened their influence.

It's been established over 15 years and it's a pretty solid club. It's an advantage in terms of its strength. It's a disadvantage in terms of breaking into it. So it's a barrier if you like from a career development point of view. (male)

So respondents recognize the importance of various non-meritocratic criteria and what might be broadly described as organizational acceptability. The importance of cultural capital as well as appropriate credentials for occupational success was understood long ago by Fromm, who argued that it was the 'personality package' based on a combination of technical skills, credential and charismatic qualities that was up for sale:

Even the best bedside manner and the most beautifully equipped office on Park Avenue would not make a New York doctor successful if he did not have a minimum of medical knowledge and skill. Even the most winning personality would not prevent a secretary from losing her job unless she could type reasonably fast. However, if we ask what the respective weight of skill and personality as a condition of success is, we find that not only in exceptional cases is success predominantly the result of skill and of certain other human qualities like honesty, decency, and integrity. Although the proportion between skill and human qualities on the one hand, and 'personality' on the other hand as prerequisites for success varies, the 'personality factor' always plays a decisive role. Success depends largely on how well a person sells himself on the market, how well he gets his personality across, how nice a 'package' he is; whether he is 'cheerful', 'sound', 'aggressive', 'reliable', 'ambitious'; furthermore, what his family background is, what club he belongs to, and whether he knows the right people. (Fromm 1949: 69–70)

Women as a sex do not fit the stereotype of management that prevails in these companies. They are usually not even considered when senior jobs are filled. Because visibility, acceptability and net-working are gendered processes, women are particularly disadvantaged in promotion procedures. The majority of women also feel that rewards are largely based upon perceptions, and that their male colleagues are particularly adept at playing the perception game – becoming much more involved internally with high-profile project work.

A theme that constantly recurs in the interviews is that women's success is severely hampered by the unconscious assumption that they do not make the right impact. Chip is described by the woman manager in charge of equality policy as having 'a particular success style, which is very high impact, quite loud, political. Less emphasis on ability to actually deliver. More emphasis on managing upwards.' By this she means:

> Crudely it's about keeping your boss happy and your boss's peers. It's managing up to those senior to you rather than managing down. So your priorities are to manage upwards. So to look good, to manage your image, the image of your department if you're responsible for a department, managing perceptions, rather than necessarily being seen as a particularly good manager by your subordinates or indeed your peers.

Another woman manager explains the problem in similar terms:

> Men will tell the board what they think the board wants to hear. Men market themselves so that whatever happens will be positive, they daren't tell any bad messages for whatever reason, either they'll get thrown out or their proposal won't get through or they'll get a bad press, whatever. They are more politically astute . . . women are more honest and direct and if there's a bad message we can't see the problem with telling it.

So managing a highly visible image with your boss is key to promotion. Men who cannot do so fail like women. The crucial problem is that the *same* behaviours exhibited by a woman are interpreted differently. For example, women who adopt a high profile are commonly regarded as 'pushy'. Moreover, women are visible in a different way by virtue of being few in number. This minority status reinforces their reluctance to pursue an approach which 'draws attention'. The behaviour of women managers continues to be seen through a gendered lens, as I elaborate in the next chapter.

This point about visibility is directly connected to one of the main findings of the survey, noted in table 4.2 above, about the existence of the 'senior management club'. Although some men also feel excluded by this club, the male-dominated senior networks are perceived to exclude females. It is the use of these 'old boy networks' to identify potential candidates for closer consideration that effectively bars women's progress at the top.

> It's always been men at the top of this company and the top of the company I was in before. They all know each other. They've all come up the same route together, all boys together. Now the only way to get into senior management is to know people in the senior management clique, but how can you know them when you are invisible? (female)

> If you're in the club then you can get entry to the more senior jobs, you can be considered for them. If you're out of the club either because you're a new person or because your face doesn't fit, whatever, then you're banging your head against a brick wall. It's based on a shared history and it's 99 per cent male. (female)

This point is clearly made by the head of career and management development at the pharmaceutical company that participated in this study. On her office wall she has a framed cartoon showing a woman and several men playing golf inside an office suite. The man is telling the woman that she'll have to improve her stroke to become a manager! This joke represents for her the lack of understanding that top management has of equal opportunity issues.

Although promotion policies at Chip mitigate overt sex discrimination, gendered conceptions about women workers as mothers still prevail and make women with children less acceptable at senior levels. Employers discriminate not simply between men and women, but between women on the basis of their actual or potential family commitments. A study of sex discrimination in the service sector identified many jobs for which employers actually preferred working wives, but concluded that there were no jobs for which being the mother of young children was seen to be an advantage (Curran 1988). What Curran calls 'familial discrimination' disadvantages mothers of young children not only relative to men, but also relative to other women. Even in progressive companies, corporate responses to family needs are constructed as special benefits rather than rights.

As a result, employees feel a low sense of entitlement to assistance with the demands of family. Although women may feel more entitled than men to make family needs visible, they do not necessarily feel entitled to both support for family care and equity in career development. Hence many career women are reluctant to take up benefits, while others accept that if they do, it will inevitably damage their careers (Lewis 1997).

At Chip, most senior women managers do not have children. Those that do often encounter prejudice:

> I went for an internal interview within the company and the guy said to me, 'you've got a young daughter', she was about six at the time, 'supposing I ask you to go to Liverpool at three o'clock this afternoon. What are you going to do about it?' I said, 'I'd get in my car and go,' and he said, 'what about your daughter?' And I said, 'well, she's cared for, I have made arrangements for her, it's no different than if somebody was to ask you to go.' I didn't get the job, and when I got the feedback about it, he said that he was concerned that my domestic circumstances wouldn't have enabled me to do the job. (female)

Such discrimination is not necessarily a conscious process but is a taken-for-granted, unexamined practice. While men may express support for equal opportunities, their prejudices are embedded in organizational rules and procedures, and in the very character of the job. The effect for women, as reflected in my interviews, is that they never seem quite right for the job, or seem not quite ready. They are too narrow in experience and they can't take the pressure. I now turn to examine the attitudes and experiences of managers to the equal opportunity policies at Chip.

Great Expectations, Realities and Resistance

As a company Chip is unusually zealous in its pursuit of innovative equal opportunity policies. Equal opportunity has a high profile within the company and generates high expectations. The continuing underrepresentation of women at senior levels within the company prompted women and men to reflect on the effectiveness of these policies.

> I think the policies themselves are probably what you'd expect and say all the right things. We all think the right things . . . I'm conscious while I say that, and it was something that came home to me in the latest

reorganization, there are no women branch managers. There must be something wrong, there must be a problem somewhere. We're now in a structure where every single branch manager is a man. (male)

Most women managers express disappointment with the lack of progress.

I think they [equality policies] are there as a stick, to say, you will do this . . . it's only if you're prepared to fight around a decision that the equal opportunities stuff gets brought in . . . I'm not sure that they do make a vast amount of difference. I don't think most people take it into account. (female)

Equal opportunity policies . . . there's a lot more talk about it. There's apparently more access to senior management to talk about it. There is a senior women's forum where our CEO speaks with women across the corporation about the issues of equal opportunities for them and how it's working out. I think he does it once a quarter. And we have a network in the UK of women who meet monthly to progress the fortunes of women in the organization. But it's all talk and I'm frustrated and a bit angry that there's no action. The senior managers' time scales for this are so far out it's never going to impact anybody in my position, it probably won't impact anybody in the company now because what they're talking about is graduate recruits into the organization who will have equal opportunities. (female)

Chip had introduced an innovative affirmative action scheme which involved financial incentives to increase the number of women in senior management. The board was required to put in place development plans for women with the potential to reach the most senior levels. Managers' goal sheets included this objective, so their management performance bonus depended on it. If they failed to reach their target, they would not receive their performance-related bonus. According to the equal opportunity officer, she had heard this referred to as a 'grab a girly programme'. But it did have a real impact during its very limited life of six months. The provision of a financial incentive did concentrate minds: 'I could tell by the level of activity, the number of calls I was getting from board members, saying, help me with this. And I thought this is wonderful, we've got it.'

Her enthusiasm was not shared by all the managers with whom I spoke, even though the scheme was limited in both time and scope. The equal opportunity officer explained to me: 'Unfortunately there was no management performance bonus paid out that year because of the business of the company. So those that were cuter and managed upwards and looked at their priorities, let it slip. But some managers did do it.'

Several men express their disquiet in strong terms:

There was an active goal for each manager to make sure that 15 per cent of his workforce are women, especially in senior levels . . . I'm against positive discrimination. Because people should get jobs based on their ability to do the work and their personality to achieve and their behaviour within an environment. It should have nothing at all to do with their sex. Idealistically it should have nothing to do with their colour either. So I totally disagree with positive discrimination because I think it undermines the success of the people who have got there without it. It was becoming so ridiculous that people with less ability were starting to get jobs. But yes I've become very cynical towards it and it didn't impact me. I could see colleagues who were a damn sight better than other colleagues being overlooked because they weren't female. And I found that to be an insult to the *people* who've been so damn successful without it and therefore not being categorized as 'one of those women who got the job because we all know why don't we'. (male)

Another male respondent, who clearly did not see it as part of his responsibility to provide support to women colleagues in difficulty, describes the scheme as destructive for women:

They chose some token women . . . they were given opportunities but it was tokenism . . . they weren't competent to do the jobs they were invited to do . . . I don't think they had the skills or the support . . . I can only speak for three of them whom I have personal contact with . . . one of them had a nervous breakdown . . . one of them just realized she was climbing the walls and got out before it happened . . . one succeeded. (male)

The other most visible positive discrimination policy tried at Chip was in relation to selection for redundancy. Chip UK was instructed by its European headquarters to ensure that women should not be selected, provided all the other criteria could be met. According to the equal opportunity officer, it caused 'a great deal of comment and cries of "foul" and "how unfair". I felt it was cathartic because redundancy's such an emotional issue, it got people out of political correctness and actually got some emotion on the table and people were able to vent it. So I think that was quite therapeutic. But it did cause quite a lot of resentment and it hasn't been repeated.'

While everyone endorses fairness to the sexes, such an affirmative direction was seen as going too far. The male human resources manager comments: 'Personally I'm a supporter of the equal opportunities stuff that we produced but I'm not a supporter of positive discrimination. One thing that hacked me off recently was when we had a redundancy exercise of top-middle management to senior manager level . . . the edict came down from Europe to say that women were not to be impacted by this. It said that we want to create a special category of person, that is women in this case. It was positive discrimination.'

This view reinforces the results of my survey reported earlier, which generally found little support for positive discrimination among men or women, although men are more likely to 'strongly disagree'. In men's view it amounts to reverse discrimination. It is those men competing for the same jobs as the women who feel (and are) most threatened by women's advances. It diminishes their advantage in the opportunity structure of the company. The few men at the top who are in effect pushing for the introduction of women as equal colleagues to more junior men are not themselves at risk. They may like or dislike the policy and its implications for fraternal solidarity, but it will not affect them personally. Men's unity is riven with fault lines, and their interests vary according to their position in the hierarchy.

Several researchers have examined organizational responses to the introduction of equal opportunities policies. In general, as we saw in chapter 1, they conclude that organizational structures either have been unaffected or have adapted and incorporated such policies with no significant changes in the gender hierarchy of organizational positions. At Chip there is no doubt that as a result of equal opportunity policies, the culture has become more receptive to women managers and that the official discourse is non-sexist. However, the fact that women's progress up the corporate ladder is far from unimpeded indicates underlying resistance and the pervasive operation of subtle exclusionary practices.

In her study of the part played by men in diverting and resisting sex equality in organizations, Cockburn describes the ways in which men are culturally active in creating an environment in which women do not flourish: 'men's discourse can be seen in many cases to cement relations among men, to put women down and to minimise the impact of the equality strategy' (1991: 66). The equality officer at Chip talks about the unconscious assumptions held by men and the 'fine line between raising the awareness so that you make them politically correct, and actually challenging their thinking and getting them open enough to reflect on what it is they're actually doing'. In the same vein, the male head of personnel explains: 'it is not OK to be sexist around here because the company's values are against that kind of thing. So what happens is, it gets driven underground.' He goes on to say that the old boy network still operated as before 'to protect men's power'.

Men's enduring problem with sex equality is the difficulty they have in maintaining their masculine identities, which are reliant on working in a male environment and doing work considered manly. Women's entry not only threatens their jobs, but their masculinity as well. It also devalues their job as such, thus further diminishing their male identity. Being a manager is about being a man and about how men view themselves. We will see in chapter 5 just how consistently men invoke a discourse of gender differentiation, defining management as intrinsically masculine and problematizing women's relation to power and authority. Although it takes a variety of forms, and varies in its intensity even within one organization, men manage to define women's difference to suit themselves.

Finally, it is clear from my research that a key factor in the durability of career ceilings for women is the business context. The current climate of almost continuous corporate restructuring and job losses has greatly intensified work for senior managers and means that opportunities for promotion for both sexes have severely contracted. In fact, the major topic of conversation among managers at the fast-contracting Chip company is the size of the redundancy package.

> If you'd walked into the office at eight o'clock in the morning 18 months ago you would have seen people working and you would have still seen them here really late at night, when their job demanded it of them. You don't see that now. The car parks are empty at six o'clock . . . and I think it's because people really felt part of a family.

> But the culture in the company at the moment is one of despair and perhaps one of inevitability that we are not fixing, things are not getting better. Things are actually getting worse and worse in almost every respect in terms of the working environment. I don't mean the physical environment, things you're expected to do and the lack of support to actually make that happen and the frustrations that are in the job because things are not done right the first time.

While insecurity about the future is pervasive, these trends have a differential impact on the careers of male and female managers. Chip was undergoing a major redundancy exercise during the period in which I carried out my research and it was evident that a disproportionately high number of the senior women were being made redundant. Men and women express somewhat different views on the extent to which this represents 'voluntary' redundancy. Men on the whole think that the few senior women are unable to take the 'increased pressure' generated by the new business context: 'the commitment that is being asked may be too much for a lot of ladies . . . not so bad for blokes cos it's expected, it's a man's thing to make sacrifices.' Another male comments:

> A lot of senior women have left . . . three senior women all on the same day . . . they were all voluntary. I think that a lot of women have found the current environment hard and simply felt: I don't think we have to put up with this any longer, I'm off. I don't think actually it's been discrimination against women. It's been an environment in which they have felt very uncomfortable.

Many women express a rather different view. They account for women's departure in terms of blocked career paths, and feel that women are pressed in various ways to accept the redundancy package:

> Well I think one of the reasons is that women who get to a senior level aren't prepared to stick around at just below the level they're looking for. I think everyone wants to believe that if they work, if they do a good job they can be promoted and if you get to a point where you feel it doesn't matter what you do you won't be promoted, then you go elsewhere.

> In the last reorganization I didn't get one of the senior jobs . . . I was offered a couple of less senior jobs and decided that actually that was probably not the right thing for my career . . . so I've been made redundant. The company is reducing in size . . . there are fewer jobs to go around. It should almost have been mandated to appoint at least one woman to one of those senior appointments because there are a lot of women in the organization, there *were* I mean. There were three or four strong candidates in my view . . . I wouldn't have been as disappointed if one of my female peers got one . . . I'm struggling with why.

As the new head of human resources explains: 'with huge job retrenchment and managers spread so thin, give me a known quality, and often the known quality to a man is another man – like hires like.' Viewing the appointment of women as a bit of a gamble, she admits that at this point she could not subject the business to that kind of risk: a perverse view for a successful woman, but she clearly sees herself as atypical.

Gendered custom and practice reassert themselves in this environment. Many of my interviewees commented that, with 'downsizing', management is returning to a more traditional hierarchical structure. Macho management is again in the ascendancy. Indeed, men's resistance to equal opportunities, which constitute a threat to their own career prospects as well as to their identities, is likely to intensify in this climate. The picture for women managers looks particularly bleak. At this stage what emerges most clearly is that women have had to become more like men to pursue successful management careers. This is a severely restricted model of equality in which it is women who must accommodate to pre-existing male norms. Relatively few women can benefit under this model.

The criterion of acceptability or the possession of appropriate cultural capital has always been important in recruiting for management. However, in bureaucratic organizations greater emphasis was placed on formal credentials and technical expertise. Evidence is now beginning to emerge that with the move to flexible corporate structures, the definition of managerial qualities may be changing. Brown and Scase (1994) suggest that increasing importance will be placed on the 'personality package' across a much broader range of management jobs, and not simply those located in the uppermost echelons of organizations. This trend comes about because the centralized forms of social control in bureaucratic organizations weaken and are replaced by new forms of motivation based on sharing corporate culture and goals. Moreover, in the context of project teams the ability to get on with others and to identify with a strong management-based corporate culture is paramount. According to the rhetoric of present-day management gurus, the post-bureaucratic organization requires managers with charismatic personalities based on personal and interpersonal skills. Such managers lead through the use of charismatic rather than bureaucratic authority. In other words, these managers inspire trust and loyalty.

As a result, the criteria for advancement become more intangible and implicit, more a matter of personal compatibility and perceptions. Smith's (1990) study of a major bank in California supports this view, arguing that senior managers in adaptive organizations are less constrained by the formal and explicit criteria regulating promotion processes than they are in bureaucratic organizations. And as personal compatibility with others becomes more important for entry and success in managerial jobs, individuals of working-class origins, women and ethnic minorities are at a distinct disadvantage. The increasing significance of cultural capital, albeit cast in a new form, reinforces social and educational inequalities.

The extent of the shift towards adaptive, flexible organizations is still very much an open, empirical question. Furthermore, it is unclear whether the changes in organizations Brown and Scase (1994) describe are dictated by exogenously driven structural changes. A combination of the oversupply of graduate labour and heightened competition for fewer places would in themselves explain employers' increasing concern both about the status of credentials and the personal qualities of the individuals possessing them. In addition, their argument about the need for charismatic leadership is far too general. Different kinds of companies may well have different tastes in the personality design of their managers.

Perhaps the most interesting feature of their thesis is that the current hyperbole about the flexible, communicative and entrepreneurial manager fits so well with the re-emergence of class-based cultural capital. The authors suggest that the celebratory rhetoric of widening access and opportunity, couched in the official discourse of educational expansion and labour market flexibility, paradoxically produces a narrowing of the social backgrounds of senior managers.

Conclusion

The data from my survey show that the few women who have succeeded in these companies are those who have very similar backgrounds and attitudes to the men. For example, they work the same long hours as men. Therefore we cannot explain women's career barriers in terms of individual characteristics like their motivation or commitment to work. Neither can women's lack of progress at senior levels be explained by their greater involvement in housework and childcare. Most of the women up against the infamous glass ceiling have already found it necessary to forgo having children.

We must therefore look elsewhere for a satisfactory explanation of women's arrested career development. I have argued that the shape of the corporate career is itself fundamentally gendered. Firstly, the classic career is predicated on the sexual contract, which supports the male life-cycle. Mothers are not seen as appropriate employees for senior management levels whereas the family man is the ideal. Family-friendly policies have been directed towards women and have not disrupted the male standard of a manager. Consequently such policies may reinforce the sexual contract by treating women as the problem.

Secondly, the effect of gendered organizational processes is to marginalize women and ultimately exclude them from the most senior management levels. Because men still define the job of manager, even if women forgo having children, all women are actively constructed as different *within* the workplace.

The companies involved in this study have exemplary equal opportunity policies. The official discourse is no longer sexist and overt discriminatory practices have been all but eliminated. Yet few women get to the top. This would suggest that company policies have been more successful in modifying managers' stated attitudes, especially men's, than they have been in transforming their day-to-day beliefs and behaviours. Certainly most men in these companies accept formal equality for women. While some men may feel threatened by women's entry, many others are comfortable working alongside women. It has become legitimate for women to hold positions of authority. Men, it seems, can no longer assume a privileged position simply by virtue of their (middle-class) male presence. The gender regime embedded in modern management is thus taking on a different hue. Some have gone so far as to declare this changed landscape of power as a post-feminist era.

Nevertheless, men as a group are managing to contain the potential erosion of their advantage. This is particularly evident in the gap between formal recruitment, selection and promotion procedures designed to ensure that appointments are made on merit, and their practical operation. These procedures have been quite effective at lower levels of organizations. Entry to senior levels however, is still heavily dependent on implicit criteria of visibility and acceptability that are, in turn, a function of the men's network. Although only some men benefit from these networks, all women are excluded.

The problem for women is that the valuing of visibility and acceptability is itself a form of gender bias. Women cannot fulfil these criteria because even when they perform in the same way, their behaviour is interpreted differently. The presence of a few senior women managers has not substantially undermined the male model of management. Indeed it appears that various forms of cultural capital – including personality and style – are becoming more salient, as corporate restructuring causes managers' career opportunities to contract. The body is also increasingly implicated in this emphasis on the presentation of self.

The premium now attached to the designer employee/personality package may well result in new forms of exclusion for women. To date, feminist commentators on organizational change have not attended to the significance of these kinds of cultural capital for the current gendering of the labour market. In the following chapter I examine how the deployment of emotions in the managerial job contributes to the contemporary character of gendered work. By doing so, I hope to make a contribution to understanding the importance of the mobilization of cultural capital in this guise for the new 'post-organization' career.

5

Personal Management: Sexuality and Workplace Relationships

This chapter examines whether men and women at the same managerial level experience organizational life differently, and how relationships at work are negotiated. Women who step outside traditional forms of female employment, such as the women managers in my study, enter a male-dominated corporate world. While both sexes are involved in presenting themselves so as to maintain an image of an authoritative manager, the sexualization of women's bodies presents a specific problem for women. In addition, the emotional dynamics of heterosexual relations involve women more in the labour of negotiation than is required of men. This means that women are saddled with more work than men simply to legitimate their presence in management. Finally, I look at how managerial succession routinely operates through affinities and alliances between men, a process that makes it difficult for women to inherit power naturally. My argument is that the way personal relationships are structured within organizations reinforces men's power. Women's bodies, like their emotional services, are an implicit part of the employment contract. But first I describe prevailing discourses about managers, as they provide the context for understanding why men's experience of relationships at work differs from women's.

Sexed Narratives about Managers

One of the major barriers facing women managers today is the continued bias against women grounded in the gendered constitution of the managerial position. With men's historical domination of management, where the vast majority of organizations have been and are still managed by men, the very notion of a 'manager' has a gendered significance. It is associated with manliness. In other words, 'think manager, think male' (Schein 1994). However, as Connell (1995) emphasizes, we need to recognize the multiple forms that masculinities and their representations take. The masculinity of corporate management can then be theorized as a specific, culturally dominant form of hegemonic masculinity.[1]

The management literature typically represents the transition to the modern bureaucratic organization as the triumph of rationality over emotion. The manager, as the exemplar of bureaucratic rationality, is the detached objective expert. 'Hegemonic masculinity establishes its hegemony partly by its claim to embody the power of reason' (Connell 1995: 164). Connell describes an important division that has developed between forms of masculinity organized around direct domination (such as corporate management) and forms organized around technical knowledge (such as the professions). The men in my study, as managers of high-technology companies, cross the divide, especially in my case study company, where the vast majority of male managers have an engineering background.

I have written elsewhere about the sense of mastery over technology and its connection with masculinity (Wajcman 1991). Of all the major professions, engineering contains the smallest proportion of females and projects a heavily masculine image hostile to women. Engineering is a particularly intriguing example of an archetypically masculine culture because it spans the boundary between physical and intellectual work and yet maintains strong elements of mind/body dualism.

Central to the social construction of the engineer is the polarity between science and sensuality, the hard and the soft, things and people. This social construction draws on a wider system of symbols and metaphors that identifies women with nature and men with culture. Sexual ideologies are diverse and fluid, but such opposites as 'male/female' and 'reason/emotion' are central to Western culture. The notion that women are closer to nature than men is taken to imply that women are more emotional, less analytical and weaker than men. In the advanced industrial world, where scientific and technical rationality are highly valued, these associations play a powerful role in the ideological construction of women as inferior. Hacker (1981) found that engineers had a clear hierarchy of social values, giving most prestige to scientific abstraction and technical competence and least to feminine properties of nurturance, sensuality and the body. Engineering seems to be the very epitome of cool reason, and the antithesis of feeling.

What is especially interesting is the way in which engineers mythologize their work in terms of the traditional 'warrior ethic' of heroic masculinity. These white middle-class men, who are far removed from any tangible physical danger, draw on the culturally dominant form of masculinity for their notions of risk, danger and virility to describe their work. In a similar vein, the men in my study readily employ military metaphors to describe their managerial work. Roper's (1994) research on the changing character of masculine authority in British manufacturing companies likewise reveals a cult of toughness and 'hard' masculinity among managers. Images of masculinity take a somewhat different form in the non-manufacturing corporate sector. Within popular culture now, it is Bill Gates as the head of Microsoft who is an icon. To be in command of the very latest technology signifies being involved in directing the future. So it is a highly valued and mythologized activity. Images of managers of high-tech companies are doubly imbued with power as they involve both mastery of technology and the control of other people. The depiction of these functions as overwhelmingly masculine may signify the emergence of a new corporate masculinity, which will present new barriers to women in management.

Women are still viewed primarily in sexual terms in our society. The problem of sexual harassment is now gaining widespread recognition, but underlying its overt expression are more subtle and pervasive processes. In *Men and Women of the Corporation* Kanter provides a classic description of how women, who are few in number among their male peers, become 'tokens; symbols of how-women-can-do, stand-ins for all women'. She argues that the strikingly uneven numerical distribution of men and women in the corporation influences behaviour in the organization and results in women being stereotyped. Men tolerate token women only so long as they are able to consign them to conventional roles that preserve familiar forms of social interaction.

Token women must be encapsulated into a category that men can respond to, understand and control. This creates informal role traps, four of which were catalogued by Kanter. They are the mother/madonna, the seductress/whore, the pet and the iron maiden. The nurturing-maternal role is that of the good listener, someone who is easy to talk to about private problems and who provides comfort. This counsellor role provides emotional services. Kanter's description has a strong resonance with recent feminist writing on women's emotional labour and conversation work, as we see below. Other women are regarded as sex objects, as sexually desirable and potentially available, and are cast as seductresses. Then there is the 'pet', someone adopted by the male group as a cute little thing, encouraged to make girlish responses and to admire male displays. Lastly, we are presented with the image of the 'iron maiden' to which strong women are consigned. If a woman refuses the first three roles, displays competence in a forthright manner, and demands treatment as an equal, she is cast as a tough women's libber and faces isolation. Whereas seductresses and pets provoke protective responses, the iron maidens 'were left to flounder on their own and often could not find peers sympathetic to them when they had problems' (1977: 236).

What Kanter highlights is the difficulty of finding a positive image of powerful women in our culture. It is striking that Margaret Thatcher, the most powerful British female politician this century, was regularly portrayed as 'not a real woman'. Powerful women are often described as aggressive and ambitious, whereas powerful men are simply considered successful. Whichever of the four stereotypes women are cast in, all disqualify them for the job of a manager. Women have to walk a tightrope between femininity, which requires them to be submissive, and masculinity, which permits them to assert authority.

If Kanter's categories seem dated one has only to glance at the many contemporary manuals on how to present for success. This 'advice' literature, described by Sheppard (1989), devotes considerable attention to controlling female sexuality. The focus is on how to create an appearance of wealth and status which conveys authority and power, while de-emphasizing sexuality. A woman's clothing must avoid drawing attention to her body, but must not ape the male business suit either. She must not be seen leaving a business meeting to go to the toilet, nor should she be seen purchasing a sanitary tampon from the women's toilets, because this action reminds witnesses she may have menstrually related moods. She should be careful that the language she uses is not about bodies. And she should be aware of the kinds of pictures she uses in her office. 'A painting of a cavalry charge or a steam locomotive would probably be too masculine: a watercolour of a meadow with a lot of pastels might be too feminine. Hang only neuter art' (Sheppard 1989: 150). The pressure for women to 'dress for success' implies they have to literally put on another mantle in order to become management material.

Although desexualization is generally perceived as a necessary protective strategy, there remains an expectation that managerial women should be pretty. Indeed, a concern with appearance, body shape and desirability has increased over the last decade or so. The ultimate accolade for a contemporary woman is that she is not only a successful career woman but attractive with it. Ironically, as Coward argues,

> women's successes in the workplace have made them ever more anxious to please men, for it is certainly the case that being sexually attractive now seems to be *de rigueur* for a successful woman. Expectations have moved very quickly from career women being 'blue-stockings' and therefore unsexy, through the acceptance of women being clever *and* attractive, to the point now where some men seem to think women are not clever *unless* they are attractive. (1993: 159)

Despite new images of women in management, they are still sexualized. This trend provides a clear connection to the general argument often made by theorists of sexuality, that there has been a relatively recent intensification of the sexualization of gender. The workplace is a central site of this sexualization.

Sexual Harassment

The construction of masculinity and femininity means that women always work as 'women' and, as such, are positioned as objects of male desire. As noted in chapter 2, organization theory increasingly acknowledges the link between sexuality and power in organizations. Male sexuality underpins the patriarchal culture of professional and organizational life. Sexuality thus becomes a crucial component of gender-power relations within workplace cultures. Feminists have written about the way men exercise control over women through both verbal and physical sexual harassment. The central argument is that theorizing male power in organizations involves seeing organizations as arenas of men's sexual dominance.

Most feminist discourse on male sexuality in organizations has focused on sexual harassment. In recent years it has been recognized that sexual harassment is a specific form of sexual discrimination in the workplace. Although the term is a relatively new one, the behaviour and injuries it encompasses are old. This form of harassment represents an expression of sexual politics at the interpersonal level and is an indication of male domination of women. Hearn and Parkin (1987) have shown how male managers routinely use sexuality, joking and abuse as a means of maintaining authority. A range of evidence produced during the last decade or so indicates that sexual harassment is a regular feature of working life for most women, though the type of behaviour to which they are subjected varies (Industrial Relations Services 1992). Sexual harassment usually involves 'unsolicited non-reciprocal male behaviour that asserts a woman's sex role over her function as a worker' (Benokraitis and Feagin 1995: 31).

The available literature suggests that women in non-traditional work are more often at risk of sexual harassment than their counterparts in traditional forms of female employment (Collier 1995; DiTomaso 1989; Hadjifotiou 1983; Stanko 1988). In a study of women managers in the UK insurance sales industry, Collinson and Collinson (1996) support this conclusion. Indeed they argue that the presence of a small number of women (token females) in male-dominated workplaces may not so much challenge as actually reinforce the dominant culture of masculinity. Their view accords with feminist theory, namely, that sexual harassment is used by men to exclude women from non-traditional work. Both Cockburn (1991) and Collinson and Collinson (1996) found that even highly qualified senior women are trapped by these highly masculine and hetero-sexualized cultures. They both report evidence of women suffering extensive sexual harassment but receiving no support from senior managers, who often saw it as women's individual responsibility to cope with sexual harassment.

Certainly many stories of sexual harassment were reported to me during my interviews. However, the most common cases were those involving managers and secretaries, where men still use their power to obtain sexual gratification from their subordinates. I briefly describe one such incident reported to me by a male human resources manager.

> He's a bit of a drinker this guy, and he asked his secretary to meet him at a pub, restaurant even, and they met and they drank a couple of bottles of wine. This guy was probably in his early fifties, I guess the woman was also in her mid-forties but very well presented was one way of describing her. And she went along to the thing and she says she didn't drink anything well believe that, maybe had a glass of wine, he had maybe one and a half bottles of wine and then said, 'oh, must call in at the golf club to sort out teeing off time for the weekend, will you

come with me,' drove up there, then in the car park suggested she hold his hand, she reluctantly did that. Then he drove to a more secluded spot where courting couples meet and grabbed her breasts.

Although the incident is typical, the response of the human resources manager is less typical. He was determined to take decisive action against the culprit, and was supported in this approach by a male colleague. However, they did not enjoy the unqualified support of their superior, illustrating the divisions that can arise between men in their response to sexual harassment.

> She explained the alleged assault and so I took that to Peter and we hauled the guy in, asked him to explain himself, didn't like his explanation, and fired him. I think it was entirely appropriate. What was really fascinating was this guy really didn't believe that he had done anything wrong. But my boss at the time allowed the guy the option to quit two or three days afterwards. He apparently said, we won't fire you if you just go quietly. Peter and I were both appalled and challenged this. He said, well the guy's been here a long time, he's obviously suffered, why should we make his plight even worse. When he goes to another company then it's not very good if he's been fired. My response was, so what. That's the price one pays for doing that.

The fact that the offending manager was forced to leave shows that Chip's progressive policies on sexual harassment, which are in part the result of it being a US-owned multinational, have succeeded. Such incidents are treated seriously by senior management. Even though the manner of his leaving is a measure of the durability of the traditional 'let's keep it hidden' attitude, there is also evidence of a new attitude among men as well as women that does not tolerate sexual harassment. Accounts of male managers sexually harassing their female peers were rare, and where this did occur it was more likely to be verbal rather than physical. The most common experiences of sexual harassment reported by women managers took the form of sexual remarks and sexual innuendos. Furthermore, the incidence of this behaviour varied between different parts of the organization.

It is important to recognize that there is more than one culture in operation at Chip. The management literature on culture generally takes the vantage point of senior management and considers 'culture' as something to be manipulated in pursuit of corporate goals. But in addition to the 'official' corporate culture promoted by top management, numerous subcultures grow up around different occupational groups and corporate interests. As in other corporations, different cultures characterize different sections of Chip, some less hospitable to women than others.

The sales function is historically sex-typed for men and is redolent with masculine traits of competitive and aggressive practices. Its culture is characterized by images of highly instrumental and predatory skills of persuasion, manipulation and persistence. At Chip the sales section was no different. It can be described as the place where the most hideous excesses took place: 'there's a lot of testosterone around in the selling world . . . these guys got big egos and big sexual appetites too . . . they talk about their conquests yeah it's much like school again.' This male respondent contrasts this setting with the all-male engineering section where 'the engineers just work all the hours God sends.' A woman told me that 'Chip UK is quite incestuous, there was a lot of affairs going on . . . they were all screwing with each other.'

Sexual references and sexual stories are standard fare on sales training courses. Women, always in a minority on such courses, often experience some kind of embarrassment or discomfort while taking them. Although most women managers will not put up with it, some women do. For example, I was told about a training course where the male trainer

> endlessly told stories about women with good legs and good boobs, and although most of the women got fed up with it, one of them thought they were hilarious. We had drinks one night and all them men drank themselves under the table including this girl, and I wasn't drinking . . . and the next day this woman really went for me and said you can't have a bit of fun drinking yourself under the table. And I said, it's women like you who are stopping women moving forward.

While most of the women managers I interviewed would stand up against sexual harassment when it occurred, this experience illustrates that it is an issue which can also divide women from each other. Women managers feel implicated in the sexual harassment of secretaries, and may be especially upset by what they regard as women's collusion in the sexualization of workplace relations. For example, one woman manager complained to me about a male manager who used to send pictures of penises to his secretary:

> you know, funny postcards . . . I threw them in the bin and the girls got them out. I said, you shouldn't be humouring him, and they said, come on it's all in good fun. It was the first time I discovered that a lot of the

secretaries and administrative women actually encourage it and find it acceptable behaviour.

If women are divided in their response to the dominant organizational culture, so too are feminists divided in their analysis of the sexual politics of organizations. Cockburn (1991) and Collinson and Collinson (1996) are pessimistic about the possibility of change. They describe the various ways that individual women managers respond to sexual harassment and how ineffective all these forms of resistance are. They argue that women are continually placed in a double bind where, regardless of how they try to cope with sexual harassment, their responses are criticized and used to legitimate the persistence of sexual harassment.

On the whole, senior women managers at Chip deal with sexually aggressive behaviour largely through humour. For example, in response to a manager who initiated very sexually explicit conversations, one woman said, 'I just joked about it, I just laughed and walked off.' A common response to men's behaviour is to adopt the male bantering style and to 'give as good as they get'. As another woman put it, when a colleague commented that her breasts were getting smaller:

> I said, 'it just absolutely fascinates me that you with your brain have actually got time to think about my tits, because the last thing that I would ever think about is your testicles.' He went bright red and the colleague who was with him said, 'I've never seen you go bright red ha, ha, ha.' And I said, 'all you have just done is made yourself look a prat.'

What is particularly interesting about Cockburn's account is her argument that 'new men', who expect and nominally welcome women in the workplace, produce a new sexual regime that also fails to provide the conditions for women's equality. Women are now expected to be as sexually combative and amusing as men, yet 'when they try to join equally in the sexual relations . . . they burn their fingers. When they ignore the sexualized culture they are in turn ignored and marginalised. When they resist it they are labelled spoilsports, lacking in a sense of humour' (1991: 156–8).

Heterosexualized Cultures at Work

Some feminist writing takes issue with the focus on sexual harassment and adopts a more positive view. In her book on secretaries,

Pringle (1988: 96) distinguishes between coercive and non-coercive heterosexuality for women in the labour market. Though she sees coercive heterosexuality as a problem, she views non-coercive heterosexuality as affording women pleasure and agency, and even argues that 'sexual pleasure might be used to disrupt male rationality and to empower women.' Her view is endorsed by Gherardi (1995: 60), who notes that the pleasures of work have been little studied. By stressing the coercive aspects of sexuality, feminist discourse helps to promote the view that there is no legitimate place for sexuality in the organization and regards sex with prudish distaste. Gherardi argues instead that it is time to admit 'that we seek erotic gratification in our work, that organizations inhabit our sexual imaginations, and that we use organizations to fulfil our sexual fantasies'.

Influenced by post-structuralism, these authors have introduced a fresh perspective. They are right to point out that the old feminist strategy of banishing sexuality from the workplace cannot be achieved. Furthermore, many women do not want sexuality or gender difference driven from the workplace. Flirting and humour help to alleviate the boredom, the alienation and depersonalization of bureaucratic processes. Organizational sexualities are intrinsically ambiguous and contradictory and, as Gherardi points out, it is often difficult to decide when sexual exploitation is taking place. As these writers argue, the focus on sexual harassment has tended to construct women as passive victims, making invisible the capacity of women to be the active subjects (rather than the passive objects) of sexual pleasure. This emphasis has struck a chord among a younger generation of feminists reacting against what they see as the traditional feminist view of women as victims of men's sexuality. They prefer to emphasize women's autonomy and resistance.

While I understand the appeal of this 'post-feminist' approach, it underemphasizes the overarching context of patriarchal power relations in the labour market. People are indeed mutually attracted at work and can enjoy eroticized relationships in this environment. However, I agree with Adkins (1995: 153) that even pleasurable sexual interactions between men and women are structured within a broader set of gender power relations. Furthermore, the possibilities for overturning sexual power will vary with the degree to which labour is sex segregated. Resisting sexual commodification is more difficult in situations where there are only a few 'token' women in the midst of a majority of men, as is the case in my study. And as already noted, women in male-dominated non-traditional work are more at risk of sexual harassment than their counterparts in traditional forms of female employment, where women tend to predominate.

The literature on 'organizational sexuality', discussed earlier in this book, attempts to understand sexuality in organizations in a much broader framework than research on sexual harassment. This new current in organizational theory highlights the connection between gender, sexuality and organizational power. It emphasizes that, as with other aspects of everyday life, the construction of masculinity and femininity 'sexes' organizational life.

This thesis has recently been developed further by Adkins (1995), who argues that women are compelled to carry out sexual servicing of men in employment situations. She maintains that feminist labour market theory has seen sexuality in isolation from the labour market and fails to recognize the way in which sexuality is written into gendered work relations. Her study of a hotel and leisure park develops her argument in greater detail. The work she describes is typical of the service sector and tourist industry, and demands 'people skills' that are primarily about the quality of social interaction with customers. Workers must be friendly, happy, caring, warm and smiling. However, Adkins found a clear differentiation between men and women workers in this context. Young men are used for certain jobs seen as requiring physical strength. The construction of women workers, by contrast, centres on visual appearance, especially appropriate clothing and appearing 'attractive and looking fresh'.

What Adkins stresses is that while women are constrained by a set of criteria relating to appearance, men are not. This constraint affects all women workers, regardless of their specific job. Furthermore, by responding to sexual innuendos and men's advances – by smiling, looking flattered and entering into the exchange – women were compelled to carry out sexual labour as a routine part of their job. The sexualization of women workers by both male customers and male co-workers is therefore, according to Adkins, an explicit part of all manner of service sector jobs:

> To be able to gain employment – that is, to exchange their labour – women have to forfeit or at least limit their ability to determine the use of their bodies. They agree to be sexual commodities for use by men. Men's bodies were not the subject of such objectification and appropriation, and so men could be said to 'own' their bodies in a way that women simply do not . . . Indeed, women's limited ownership of their bodies in the context of service employment relations, through bodily commodification, clearly constitutes a way in which women are not

'workers' in the same way as men, in that it shows, once again, that the conditions attached to the exchange of labour power in tourist service jobs are quite different for men and women. (1995: 159).

Thus women's bodies are an implicit part of the employment contract.

The importance of understanding the use of bodily gesture, appearance, facial expression and speech in face-to-face interactions can be traced back at least to Goffman (1967). Classic interactionist studies throw light on the nature of social interaction in day-to-day life, and show how the regulation of bodies is a requirement of most forms of work. Goffman employs the dramaturgical model to demonstrate how sensitive people are to how they are seen by others, and the way they use 'impression management' to ensure that others react in ways they wish. He shows how social life depends upon subtle relationships between what we convey with our face and bodies and what we convey in words. Reminiscent of this earlier work, feminists have begun to refer to 'gender as a performance' and 'gender as a doing' in order to stress that gender is not fixed in advance of social interaction but is constructed *in* interaction (see, for example, Butler 1990).

Organizations are one crucial site in which the doing of gender is routinely accomplished. However, as I have emphasized throughout, the high visibility of senior women managers increases awareness of their gender and means that the few women who rise to this level feel under greater pressure to perform than men. The significance of a woman's sex for both how she operates and how she is responded to tends to be scrutinized in a way that 'normal' gendered hierarchical relations are not. Given that the rules of interaction in the workplace are male, women managers are always in a precarious position trying to negotiate the contradictory demands of being feminine and being businesslike.

The management of women's self-presentation thus takes place within a context of a male-defined set of norms and expectations. In order to be successful, women managers have to employ deliberate strategies of gender management in order to 'balance the conflicting statuses of female and manager' (Sheppard 1989: 145). Without constant vigilance regarding gender self-presentation, they run the risk of not being treated seriously as managers. Although men are also involved in the presentation of self at work, as will become clear shortly, women's physical appearance is more closely regulated than men's and demands a lot more effort.

I think men have it a lot easier because they can wear a standard suit and if they wore the same suit every day of the week nobody would notice. Women have to wear different things. I couldn't wear the same dress two days running. I would wear a suit or a dress and jacket for a customer meeting, or if I was going to a meeting with senior managers in the organization. (female)

In my interviews, the question of whether it is possible to present oneself both as a competent manager and as feminine at the same time elicited some strong responses. One woman manager said:

I have had so many comments about how I look within Chip that it's not true. I used to wear my hair up, I thought that was the right image for a woman in business . . . I got some feedback from one of my managers, and he said, 'well, you do look awfully severe. Why don't you wear your hair down, long and flowing' . . . I tried this and about 20 men stopped me in the first week and said 'oh you look so lovely with your hair down.' So, I had the hair back up immediately. Some days I wear it down and I always get a comment. I can't decide whether that's nice because the men think I look lovely versus austere. So I'm in a complete dilemma about how I should wear my hair.

Addressing the same question, a male manager rehearsed the following anecdote:

I worked in America with a lot of Americans and my picture of an American manager, female manager, is again the stereotype of somebody who's had to really work so much harder to get into those positions, that has to be more masculine in the management style. Not in looks and anything else but the management style. And I was at a dinner table years ago and this wonderful Italian sales manager, lady, she just ripped this American lady apart at the dinner table by making the point that a good manager will use all they have to as a tool. And she wasn't suggesting that she used her sexuality but that she used her femininity. I mean she was a stunningly sexually attractive woman as well. But she somehow hid that in her mannerism. When she was being a manager the sexuality vanished but the femininity didn't.

In both these examples the message is that women who dress to neutralize their femininity present too powerful an image of a woman to be acceptable to men. Men prefer a visually softer, more sexual image of a woman. The woman wearing her hair up is making a statement that she intends to be businesslike. She is not interested in being the object of the male gaze, but wishes to be dealt with primarily as a fellow manager. The response of her male colleagues impels her to wear her hair down, making her a woman again by stripping her of professional authority and allowing conventional sexual power relationships to reassert themselves.

Feminist literature has properly stressed that the construction of women workers, in contrast to men, centres on visual appearance. However, while it is certainly the case that women's appearance at Chip is closely regulated, so too in its own way is men's. All the men I interviewed were well presented and several spoke to me about the importance of their image:

> Well I think it's important that you have an aura of being respectable, of being successful and being confident. A lot of that can come from the way you dress and the way that you choose the things you wear. With customers and at work as well. I think the impact that you have within a meeting with a team can often be dependent on how good you feel about yourself and therefore what you're wearing.

> Actually when I was dealing with the university sector I used to dress down. I used to wear the same suit and make it look tatty. I try and match, it's a selling thing.

> It's still the way that people assess each other . . . I'm British and I've been brought up in that way. One chap that worked for me was grossly overweight, wore terrible greeny browny suits with brown shoes that weren't particularly smart, his stomach was always hanging over his belt showing the vest he wore underneath it. He was trying to teach sales-men and rapport building. I discussed it with him and he was absolutely stunned. 'Good god it's the first time anybody has told me what the impact is,' he said.

Men in the corporation are increasingly self-conscious about their image. However, the difference is that they are not under pressure to neutralize their sexuality or disguise their bodies in the way that women are. This is so because it is the male body that is inscribed within the managerial function. 'The cult of toughness does not con-fine itself to the language which industrial managers use to describe their work; it is also conveyed in postures, gestures, facial expres-sions, and movements . . . the bodily living-out of masculine identi-ties' (Roper 1994: 108).

Negotiating Labour

As we have seen, one of the ways that women's experience of work differs from men's is the extent to which they have to redefine and

As Hochschild (1983) argues, emotional labours simply reinforce gender segregation since they involve women caring for people's immediate needs in the workplace as well as in the home. Women's emotional and expressive skills, which are exercised in the traditionally female 'caring' professions, leave them stigmatized as more emotional and dependent than the male. These skills may be appropriately exercised by nurses in hospitals or even by secretaries in firms (Pringle 1988), but not by women in management. The problem for women in management is that the role of providing emotional support, like a mother or a wife, precludes effective job performance and confirms women's subordination.

Conversational analysts have pointed out that men tend to speak differently from women, not in an absolutely predictable pattern but as a matter of degree. Women use the interrogative form more and give more listening responses. According to Tannen (1993), women and men are socialized to different discourse strategies, and this gives rise to a symmetrical misunderstanding between the sexes. She contrasts males' impersonal mode of public sphere 'report-talk' with the 'rapport-talk' through which females seek emotional connectedness in the private sphere. This way of speaking and deferential listening is the normal expectation to which most women conform.

It is very often the task of women to develop communicative competence in male discourse, to take responsibility for repairing the embarrassment caused by their difference, and to make amends for the intrusiveness of their presence.

> I was brought in to integrate two separate parts of the company and they didn't know what to do with me. They were ex-engineers and I was a woman and I wasn't interested in cars or anything they talked about. I was a complete oddity . . . my message was to make friends with them so I had to start talking about things that didn't particularly interest me . . . Now one thing I am very strong on, is that I always remember something about somebody, you know whether they were wallpapering a house the last time we spoke. So that's how I made friends. And if I wanted them to do something for me I had to have a bit of a lovely chat on the phone, talk to them for ten minutes about what kind of a day they'd had . . . and I found that all a complete waste of time but I did find it worked.

For women in senior management, who step outside the boundaries of their appropriate work status, managing interpersonal relations at work is thus an especially fraught process. They have to work hard to avoid letting the tone of domestic relationships shape those of the workplace. If women do place more importance on relationships at work than men it is not a result of their nurturing tendencies or their need for a warm supportive environment. It is, as Marshall says, because their attention is necessarily 'directed towards making potentially difficult relationships work and towards safeguarding their power and effectiveness' (1995: 195). Similar demands are not made on the time and emotional energy of male managers.

Mentoring Relationships

I have written above, in the chapter on the corporate career, about the gap between formal selection procedures and implicit criteria of acceptability in determining success at Chip. I talked there about the significance of informal social networks for gaining organizational power. I reported on responses to a number of questions in the survey which address the theme of career progression, and noted that nearly twice as many women as men say they have experienced barriers in their career. Table 4.2 (see p. 88) shows that one of the principal career barriers identified by both men and women is the lack of formal career guidance. This complaint is particularly striking, given that the companies in the survey have well-developed human resources policies. It points to the crucial significance of informal mentoring relationships in determining career progress.

In answer to a survey question about where respondents got the most positive support in their careers, both men and women mention partners, a male boss, and colleagues (see table 5.1). While many more women (22%) than men (8%) mention a female boss or role model, it is the assistance of a male boss that is decisive for both sexes. I defer consideration of the importance of partners for managers' careers until the next chapter.

What I want to examine in more detail here is the way the gender dynamics of social life at Chip disadvantage women. The way in which gender shapes the quality of everyday relationships at work has profound implications for the career development of women. Support and sponsorship from a male boss are crucial for the advancement and promotion of both men and women in organizations. For women, who are largely excluded from informal systems based largely on male meanings, mentors can help them learn about this largely 'foreign' culture (Marshall 1984: 107). The difficulty for women in access to successful mentoring relationships is that there are so few women at the top to act as sponsors for women lower down

Fortunately for me my manager also acts as my mentor. When I arrived at Chip I was officially given a mentor who really didn't do very much at all for about six months. He took quite a passive role . . . I used to just go and chat with him. He has since done lots for me over the last seven years. So now we have a *relationship* where I guess we look after each other rather than him mentoring me.

A male social world did exist within and outside work at Chip. For example, men valued socializing, meeting for a drink or over a meal at the pub, such venues often providing the context in which mentoring takes place.

I've had a pint at lunchtime, he wanted to go over the road . . . something he wanted to talk to me about, so I suppose I was in the role of a mentor. It would be more unusual for a woman to have asked me to go over to the pub at lunchtime. Women are extremely welcome to do those things, but then basically behaviour changes a little bit.

For career advice it could be anyone . . . it's typically men because it's typically men that are in management positions or at the same level as myself . . . there are lots of coffee machine conversations. In the group I am actually working with there's one woman, but the people that come to me for advice on careers are mainly men.

Men who do not participate fully in the networking also suffer the consequences:

I've fallen foul of that issue quite dramatically in the past two years. I found out that some of the people I thought were with the direction, weren't, and were doing other things behind the scenes. After we did a sensing exercise a lot of people sought me out and said: 'you haven't been around enough for the past year, you're not there at the coffee machine, you're not having lunch, you need to be doing more work informally.'

Women recognize the importance of these contacts as sources for acquiring important information, but talk about the difficulty of fitting in with this male culture.

You've got to be one of the boys . . . I don't mind going down to the pub with the boys . . . I don't get offended by the jokes . . . that's how you get to the top . . . you start to see the breaks or where something's not going quite right and you make use of it . . . I personally don't like playing that game. It's not worth the hassle.

Although many women recount stories of exclusion, others speak of the necessary assistance that male managers have given them during their careers. However, it appears to the woman quoted below that the very qualities that enable these 'liberated' men to work well with women are not the qualities of those who make it to the top.

> My first role models were not women, they were men who nurtured me in my career . . . who were definitely not threatened by me, who I found to be liberated men. When you get to the top those kind of men seem to have fallen by the wayside somewhere, and quite frankly many of the men at the top are not appealing. They are not people I would want as friends. I find that women like me are threatening to them, they much prefer to find subservient women as their partners.

> I used to have a mentor but not any more, my career actually plateaued out when I didn't have a mentor. I haven't really got anyone to turn to now. He was a man, he was my manager, we used to have terrible rows but there was a level of respect.

Some women allude to the importance of women role models and mentors. The way in which women describe these relationships is consistent with several surveys which suggest that women are more likely than men to want emotional support from a mentor, while men value the career development aspects of the relationship (Arnold and Davidson 1990).

> I lost most of my women mentors. I used to talk to them a lot, but they have gone and for a long time I was really working in isolation. I wanted to have women friends and there weren't any.

> I have two women peers. Occasionally we'll just ring up and say 'let's have a girlies lunch.' We just sit and have a whinge about how difficult it is, nobody understands how precious we are to each other.

As a way of substituting for informal male mentoring networks, a women's network was formally set up at Chip to provide support for women. However, it was not attractive to all women and it was not without its conflicts. For example, I was told that it suffered from internal friction caused by the different needs of more junior women and the senior women. The woman in charge of equal opportunity policy at Chip spoke about the diversity of political approaches used by different women.

6

Managing Home Life

In recent years much has been made of the emergence of new egalitarian forms of marital partnership involving a more equitable distribution of domestic work. The recasting of traditional gender roles and a reshaping of the family are said to be the result of women's increased labour force participation, combined with the profound cultural shift brought about by the women's movement. One might expect that women at the top of the social structure, that is women who are gaining access to professional and managerial employment, would be at the forefront of these changes. Although these women still represent only a small proportion of senior management, they hold jobs that allow them access to considerably more organizational power and economic resources than most women in the paid labour force. This chapter goes beyond the workplace to explore the domestic lives of men and women managers. My aim is to examine the domestic basis for the managerial career, and to ask whether women's power at work translates into power at home.

It is at the interface between home and work that gender differences are most stark. The data reveal that the domestic arrangements necessary and sufficient to sustain the life of a senior manager are very different for men and women, giving the lie to the myth that equality has been achieved. The problem was summed up by one woman saying: 'We all need a wife but they only come in one sex.' My basic argument is that, for all the company initiatives designed to promote equal opportunities, the managerial career is still largely dependent upon the services of a wife at home. Indeed, it presupposes a male worker 'freed' by the sexual contract. Before going on to analyse the results of my study, we need first to engage some of the debates about the relationship between family and work.

The Symmetrical Family Revisited

When feminist sociologists began analysing women's work in the 1970s, a central concern was the relationship between the sexual division of labour at work and that within the household (Barrett 1980; Beechey 1978; Wajcman 1981). We argued that one could not understand either women's or men's position in the labour market, let alone their experience of work, without examining their domestic lives. Women's primary responsibility for domestic duties meant that they were generally limited to part-time work, especially once they had children. Men were seen as the breadwinners, working full-time outside the home, and therefore doing little domestic labour. Whereas men's gender identity was primarily derived from their job, women's was said to be based on their roles as wives and mothers. There was a symbiosis between these work patterns and the patriarchal family form.

The crucial significance of the work–family nexus is widely acknowledged, although even today few sociologists of work and employment examine it in any detail. Most industrial relations studies still show little consciousness of life beyond the factory gates. Furthermore, increasing academic specialization within sociology has led to something of a separation between studies in the sociology of the family and those that deal with paid work (Cockburn 1985, 1991; Walby 1986). Within organizational sociology, feminist research has tended to move away from explanations in terms of the sphere of reproduction, focusing instead on how the gender relations of employment are produced at work. As we have seen, there has been a burgeoning literature on women in management, dealing with career structures, occupational stresses and organizational barriers. Increasingly, even studies of sexuality in the workplace tend to be divorced from any analysis of gender power relations in the home (Hearn et al. 1989; Pringle 1988). This chapter returns to earlier feminist concerns with the mutual shaping of paid work and home or family life. Now, however, I am intent on showing the centrality of this dynamic for men, as well as women.

Alongside the concern with equal opportunities in employment there has arisen a perception that the family has become more egalitarian. Indeed, there has been a significant shift in the ideology

The idea is taking hold that men are striving for a new balance between work and family, and are seeking satisfaction in 'pure relationships' rather than commercial or professional ones. Writing on love and intimacy, social theorists such as Giddens (1992) and Beck and Beck-Gernsheim (1995) draw a strong connection between the general emancipatory thrust of modernity and the new democratic politics of the private sphere. Although pioneered by women, the search for self-identity through the pure relationship, characterized by an emotional openness and intimacy associated with social and sexual equality, is now being pursued by men as well. Work as a source of self-identity has begun to fail them.

In this vein, Pahl's (1995) study of successful people concentrates exclusively on the emotional lives of male managers. It is preoccupied with their anxieties rather than with the actual character of their domestic and personal lives. Whereas the emphasis in Scase and Goffee's earlier book, *Reluctant Managers* (1993; first published in 1989), is on the identity crisis caused by the collapse of the predictable and secure managerial career, Pahl primarily attributes the malaise among successful men to the sexual revolution. He sees men as caught up in the momentum of the 'flight from patriarchy'. From the perspective of established middle-age, they regret their self-imposed exile from family life and their lack of intimacy with wife and children. When questioned about their attitudes, Pahl discovered that men rate family as more important to them than work.

But how profound is this change? Attitude surveys for a long time have found that men, like women, put home first. From Dubin (1965) through to the *Affluent Worker* studies (Goldthorpe et al. 1969), sociologists have 'discovered' that male workers rate a good family and home life as more important to them than work. Instead of taking such responses at face value, we need to explore what they really mean. Scase and Goffee describe their middle managers as being less psychologically immersed in their occupations: 'managers' personal identities are no longer solely derived from their jobs but, instead, are also shaped by a variety of non-work factors' (1993: 180). But while they say they increasingly value personal and family relationships, these men are working harder and longer than ever before. Pahl's more senior workaholic male managers express similar sentiments.

How do we account for this apparent disjunction between beliefs about the value of personal relationships and what these men actually do? This rhetoric of regret about missing out on family life has become the standard discourse about men in an age where the cultural ideal of marriage takes an intimate, companionate form. The new, more androgynous, self-reflexive male has feelings and wants to express them. The problem, according to Pahl (1995: xii), is that men are emotionally disabled, ill-prepared to achieve the balance that they so desire, a balance which would allow 'the expression of emotion or love to be combined with the development of instrumentality in employment'.

The issue is whether these men would make different choices if they had the chance. Indeed, now that they are in positions of power, they could change the structure of work so that younger men are not forced to repeat the same pattern. Talking about emotions and identities is not the same as experiencing them or taking steps to achieve a better balance. The flourishing ideology of personal growth may serve as a particularly effective way of avoiding experience of the self. As Connell points out, the attempt to remake men's identity in terms of emotional autonomy may represent containment, not revolution, in relation to the patriarchal gender order. 'The political risk run by an individualized project of reforming masculinity is that it will ultimately help modernize patriarchy rather than abolish it' (1995: 139). After all, postmodern, flexible capitalism needs postmodern flexible identities, not the old masculine organization man!

Although the analysis of gender relations is central to his thesis, Pahl's avoidance of the extensive empirical sociology on the operation of power and inequality in marriage is remarkable. Children and housework are only mentioned in an aside, where Pahl doubts 'if most male managers really want to spend their time ferrying their children to music lessons or trying to get cat sick off the carpet' (1995: 54). Perhaps if he had pondered longer on this issue, he would have come closer to answering the question with which he opens his book: 'why do men work long hours, saying that they do it for their families, when their wives or partners frequently say that they would like to see more of them?'

A dramatically different picture of the joys of worldly success is portrayed by Kanter (1989). She argues that the post-entrepreneurial corporation has increased the lure of work. Indeed, she explicitly criticizes psychological theories that see workaholics as pathological victims of the 'greedy organization'. Managers' jobs are increasingly complex, requiring high discretion to choose between options, and creativity to seize the new opportunities that are available. Such work is intellectually absorbing and immensely exciting, offering 'the exhilaration of living on the edge'. When work is so consuming, particularly in mixed-sex settings, the workplace becomes the site for intense

off between paid employment and reduced domestic labour carried out by women. Despite their power in the organization, women managers are no better off than their sisters in more lowly occupations or those who are not in the workforce at all, whose share of domestic work is similar (Gershuny et al. 1994).

However, aggregate housework figures do not fully convey the real diversity in the domestic situations of the men and women managers. The other key factor in understanding the allocation of housework is the employment status of partners, as shown in figure 6.2. Let us look first at the male managers. Only 7 per cent of the men are single or divorced. Of respondents with partners, the highest proportion (40%) have full-time housewives at home. Thirty-one per cent of men have partners who work part-time. Only a minority (27%) of men have partners who are employed full-time, that is, are living in dual-career families.

The picture for the women managers is very different. Over a quarter (27%) of women are living on their own (17% are single and 11% are divorced). Most other women are in dual-career families. Of respondents with partners, 88 per cent of women have partners who are employed full-time. Of the remaining 12 per cent of respondents with partners, a tiny number of women report having husbands who work part-time or who are at home full-time (for example, retired).

In other words, the women and men managers generally live in different types of household. Given these stark differences, it is most useful to analyse domestic work in relation to the type of family

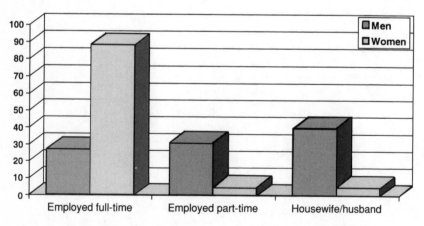

Figure 6.2 Employment status of managers' partners

respondents actually live in. Table 6.1 analyses the amount of time spent on housework by managers and their partners. The most striking feature of the survey data is that typically successful managerial careers can draw upon extensive domestic support at home. For most managers, who are men, this support comes in the form of a wife. In answer to the question 'who organizes the housework in your house on the whole?' many men instantaneously replied, 'oh, my wife.' As we can see from figure 6.2, an unusually high proportion of senior male managers have full-time housewives at home. Based on the male managers' estimates, these housewives do at home the same average weekly hours of work as their husbands do in the office – 51 hours – the equivalent to a full-time job of a senior manager! In addition, nearly a third of the men have wives who work part-time for pay, and these women also put in hours of housework equivalent to a full-time job. It follows that most of the male managers (71%) have the services of a full-time housewife, even when the wives actually have a part-time job. It is this domestic support that enables men to have children without jeopardizing their careers. Only a minority of the men do not have a partner. Most of these are divorced, suggesting that they may have built their careers on a wife's labour. Men's careers are underpinned by the domestic labour of their wives.

Table 6.1   Hours spent on housework by managers

Family type	Men	Men's partners	Women	Women's partners
Dual-career family (i.e. both employed full-time)	9[a]	19	20[a]	11
Manager with partner employed part-time	9	34	–	–
Manager with partner not employed (i.e. full-time housewife)	11	51	–	–
Single/divorced manager	9	–	15	–

Housework is defined as cooking, cleaning, laundry, shopping and childcare.
[a] Respondents with children reported more hours of housework, the women 34 hours and the men 14 hours.

towards equality within couples in terms of occupational standing, very substantial inequalities in earnings between partners remain. Only 11 per cent of married women who work full-time have higher earnings than their husband, compared with the 63 per cent of husbands who earned more than their wives. Despite a quarter-century of equal pay legislation, wives who earn more than their husbands are rare. The authors conclude that until women have higher earnings than their partners, it is unlikely that the patriarchal domestic division of labour will be seriously challenged.

This analysis of income inequality within marriage sheds light on the earlier discussion of the gendered character of housework. In 'The domestic labour revolution: a process of lagged adaptation?' Gershuny et al. are left 'puzzled' by the fact that husbands of full-time employed women still do a substantially smaller proportion of the total work of the household (1994: 179). As an answer, they invent the process of 'lagged adaptation', meaning that households adapt gradually. They assume that slowly, but inevitably, men's involvement in domestic labour will catch up with the change in paid work patterns. No mention is made by these authors of patriarchal economic power in the home and the privilege men enjoy as a result of the current organization of housework. Arber and Ginn's findings alert us to the fact that economic inequality between husbands and wives persists and this may help to explain the continuing imbalance in men's domestic contribution.

What the data reveal is a gender-segregated pattern of partnerships. In my sample, the incidence of dual-career families is very different for the men and women. A dual-career partnership for women managers comes at the cost of motherhood whereas a dual-career partnership among male managers is the exception rather than the rule. In this high modernist era, it is still the case that male managers live in families with a traditional division of labour.

Fewer than a third of the men actually have wives who are working full-time and are pursuing their own career. Even these men leave most of the responsibility for domestic work, as well as the labour itself, to their wives. Male managers in dual-career families are in fact doing less than half the housework hours of female managers in dual-career families. Although 63 per cent of the men describe their partners as having career jobs, 91 per cent of the men earn much more than their partners and, as figure 6.3 shows, most of the men's wives are in lower-grade professional/administrative occupations or in routine clerical, sales and non-manual jobs.

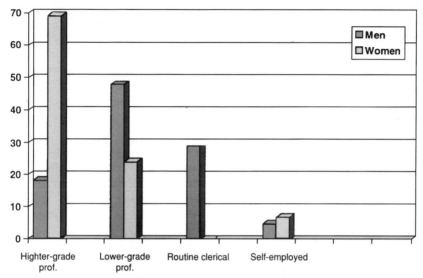

Figure 6.3   The occupations of managers' partners

This pattern is in sharp contrast to most of the women in the sample. The women's partners are overwhelmingly in higher-grade professional, managerial and administrative occupations which have traditionally been perceived to have good career prospects. Most of the women (88%) describe their partners as having a career job, and only a third said that they earn much more than their partners. More commonly, women report earning the same or just a bit more than their husbands. Interestingly, their earning power is not reflected in the domestic division of labour. Indeed, and this is particularly the case where there are children in the household, these women do over twice as much housework as their partners. So they are constantly juggling housework and paid work in a way that men are able to avoid.

Mothers are also the ones who are most likely to bring tasks home from the workplace. Whereas having children did not affect where men did their work, it did affect women. The amount of work done at home by women with children far exceeds that done by women without children. Sixty-two per cent of women with children do up to 10 hours of work per week at home. Whereas women without children tend to work long hours at the workplace, like men, mothers take more work home because of their domestic commitments.

(Adler and Izraeli 1994). The number of women sent on foreign assignments is extremely small. My research findings are consistent with those of the National Health Service study, that the mobility of women managers, while high, is not as high as men's.

Respondents in my study were asked whether the location of their house was chosen primarily on the basis of their own career or their partner's. Twice as many men (48%) as women (22%) report that their own career determined the location of their home. About half (48%) of the women managers said their domestic location was chosen jointly with their partner. Of the people who moved house for career reasons, 48 per cent of men and 27 per cent of women have moved house three or more times. This level of mobility, with all the disruption to family ties, friendships and community networks, and children's schooling, is not conducive to settled family life. As one man said, the pressure of moving was a contributing factor to his divorce:

> Commitment to work was quite a major factor in my divorce. I moved up to Aberdeen from Edinburgh, that's when I was married. When I'd been there for three years the company was reorganizing and my boss asked me to talk to my wife about the possibility of moving back home again. She was happy, although she liked Aberdeen she was happy with that because that was back to her family. And then the reorganization happened and the company basically wanted me to move to Leeds. And the way it was put to me was, 'we need to move to Leeds and I need an answer, now.' 'What's the options?', I asked. 'Well there's none really.' Now that never helped our marriage, that was like moving to an area where my wife never wanted to move in the first place. And then we split up.

Other men spoke of their increasing reluctance to move when they reached a stage in the life-cycle where family commitments impinge more forcefully: 'I was not prepared for example to move all over the country and take my kids out of school just to perhaps get a better job somewhere.'

Mobility presents a different sort of problem for managers, mainly women, who live alone. As one woman said:

> I was never able to convince the company that moving is very difficult for a single person as opposed to a family. When you move a family you have stability, whereas as a single woman on your own, it's very hard to get to grips with a new community.

Some managers had enjoyed a spell in company headquarters in the US, which is seen as a prime training ground for furthering their careers. One man lamented the loss of an opportunity to remain in US headquarters and thereby enhance his career. He was still upset when I interviewed him about having given up, for the sake of his family, what may have been a big promotion:

> I believe that I would be in a different position now if I had not come back from the States. I was there for four years and my boss tried to persuade me to stay. But no, my wife really didn't want to so we came back. That hurt me to some extent emotionally. I mean, we made the decision together and I would never have backed off that, but it hurt for the first eighteen months to two years I was back.

This scenario was relatively unusual, as women managers are in fact much more likely than their male counterparts to have the location of their employment determined by their partners. It is striking that even a senior woman who is managing a major engineering project for the company says this.

> That particular move was based on my partner's career. I like managing his career as well as my own. It's sometimes easier to manage people than to do it yourself. The other thing is that I really need him to be excited about his job. I'm not that ambitious about my career right now. My career is important . . . I have to be happy with it. But my relationship is more important.

Living in dual-career families, most women managers must accommodate the demands of their partner's career as well as their own. When it comes to management of the household, a number of strategies are available to these women, the most common of which involves hiring domestic help.

Paid Domestic Services

Recent research indicates that contracting out housework is a growing trend in Britain. Gregson and Lowe (1994) suggest that there has been a dramatic expansion in the demand for and utilization of waged domestic labour specifically by high-income, dual-career, middle-class households during the 1980s. This phenomenon has received remarkably little attention, largely because sociological research on

Even so, women with children generally stress the difficulty of reconciling home and work. For example, one woman said: 'It's a constant juggling act. Lose a nanny and life falls apart . . . The most stressful thing I found about having children is getting the right nanny and keeping her.' Another added:

> Seems to me there are three elements to life, family, social life and work. In a two-career family, one element has to go, and for me it is social life. When I am not at work, I am a full-time mother and when the children go to bed, I collapse!

It is worth noting that in all cases it is the women and not their partners who both organize and pay for domestic help. Women continue to have the responsibility for domestic work, as is illustrated in the following quotes from women managers:

> If you ask the nanny who's her boss, she'll tell you it's me. And I tend to keep in better contact with her on details, she tends to talk to me more than she'll talk to my husband. But that's partly because he forgets that I don't know things. So he forgets to pass on some of the information and she finds herself telling both of us, so it's easier just to tell me.

> Basically all our money is in joint names, we have two joint accounts and can both sign on them. I tend to take care of the nanny side and pay everything to do with that. I don't say it just comes out of my salary, our salaries get pooled. I worry about doing all the tax and national insurance for the nanny and worry about all the paper work, making sure she gets paid on time, that she gets the housekeeping allowance. And the cleaning and gardening and stuff. My husband makes sure the mortgage gets paid and all the bills . . . he likes doing that.

> I had an ironer before I had a cleaner, it was something I hated doing and I didn't have enough time. I have an ironer and a cleaner and a live-in nanny. We eat convenience food most of the week and we try and eat decent food, which my husband cooks, at the weekend and the cost of all that, our outgoings are phenomenal. I have a live-in nanny because my hours are so unpredictable and I pay for out of my taxed income her national insurance and tax and for the cleaner and ironer.

Even when the actual expense is shared, it is women who manage the often complex paid domestic labour arrangements. Men generally do not undertake this kind of managerial work at home. Male managers seem to lose their capacity to manage paid labour when it comes to domestic services at home.

Given that men generally neither do housework nor organize other people to do it, it is notable that so many women are enthusiastic about the encouragement they receive from their partners to pursue their careers. For example, one woman, describing how her retired parents pick the children up from school and look after them in the school holidays, said that her husband had never done any childcare. What support he did provide for his wife remains a mystery but she was very appreciative nonetheless.

> He leaves home at 6 am and gets home at 8.30 pm because he works in London. I get home 7.30 pm I suppose, it depends, I got home about 9 pm last night. If I am working on a big project it could be the early hours of the morning . . . He is very supportive, he understands what my job involves . . . we have a firm partnership.

Another woman described her partner in similar terms, and was especially appreciative of the absence of any conflicts about her working at home in the evenings and weekends: 'both of you are professional and you understand it . . . He's always very supportive, not the individual sort of day-to-day things but very supportive in what I want to do.'

These quotes are indicative of the low expectations women have about their partner's practical contributions and their own acceptance of most domestic responsibilities. Given such expectations, women experience their husbands as supportive simply if they are willing to accommodate a career wife. There is an evident reluctance on the part of these women to confront the fact of inequality within the home (Brannen and Moss 1991), perhaps because women do not straightforwardly judge the asymmetrical division of family work to be unfair.

The literature on domestic labour implicitly assumes that because women spend much more time on housework than men, they will resent their partners. Drawing on the idea of distributive justice to explore this issue, Thompson (1991) proposes that a sense of injustice depends upon having a high standard for comparison. Reminiscent of Runciman's (1966) classic concept of relative deprivation, this approach highlights the importance of considering to whom partners compare themselves when judging the fairness of family work. Almost all of the research on the division of domestic work assumes that the partner is the comparator and the benchmark is a 50–50 split (that is, equality). However, Thompson suggests most women compare themselves with other women rather than to men, and this reference undermines any sense of entitlement. As Hochschild (1990) discovered, many women use the ideal of the 'superwoman' and compare how much they should accomplish relative to other energetic, organized women. They also make within-gender comparisons of their husbands. Comparing their husbands with other men, who may do even less around the house, they judge their own circumstances as not so bad. Women would have a stronger sense of injustice about family work if they compared themselves to their husbands.

Furthermore, what women want from their domestic arrangements is not adequately captured by measuring the distribution of time and tasks. Thompson (1991) argues that women value interpersonal outcomes more than time and tasks, and that their sense of justice rests more firmly on the distribution of these valued outcomes. Feeling that their husbands understand their problems and are responsive to their needs is what matters to them. For example, Backett (1987) found that if husbands listen to their wives talk about the children and give their wives occasional respite from minding the children, then wives believe husbands are involved fathers – even if the men rarely do any childcare. Wives tend to overlook injustice if they believe that their husbands provide care and communication. They are more concerned about the expressive or emotional qualities of their relationships, such as love and intimacy, than with the instrumental aspects of work tasks. This tendency is probably accentuated in more affluent families, where women have the option of buying themselves out of a good deal of this domestic work.

Viewed from yet another perspective, women might be interpreted as being complicit in maintaining traditional family structures and expectations. Using a psychoanalytic framework, Coward (1993: 120) reports of the middle-class women she interviewed: 'far from listing men's inadequacies, [women] seem pathetically grateful for any small amount of domestic input. And many still seem to partake of "the exempted man" syndrome identified by feminism many years back – all men are dreadful except the one you happen to live with.' She argues that women tend to idealize their male partners and have a much deeper fear of challenging men in their private lives than in the public world. Although I disagree with Coward's emphasis on women's culpability rather than on men's resistance, we do need to ask, as she does, 'why do women let men get their way.'

Men are similarly adept at avoiding the issue of domestic inequality. They too perceive their partner's career support primarily in emotional rather than practical terms:

My partner gives me a lot of support. We discuss not so much the work, more the people associated with the work. My wife is a trainee Relate counsellor. I think she's got, not a more sensitive, but a more appreciative dimension for looking at aspects like feelings, motivations and all those kinds of things, than frankly I have. So just by talking over some of the people-type situations I can get a lot of value and support from that.

She's incredibly supportive. If I want to talk about it, she'll listen. She never makes any judgements and if I decide to do something, she thinks it's a good idea and supports what I've done. But she doesn't ask until I say.

I tend not to speak about day-to-day issues. You know, what sort of day did you have today, and go into detail about what I've done. I choose the issue quite carefully. But issues like, I've got to make someone redundant tomorrow or I can't understand what the hell we're doing at the moment, we talk through issues like that. We talk about my work but it's not a dominant conversation topic unless there's something going on at that particular time.

Writers such as Giddens and Pahl wrongly assume that intimacy in heterosexual couples is based on a mutual recognition of the need to share domestic tasks. What they rightly emphasize, however, is that modern marriage has come to be increasingly interpreted in idealist romantic terms rather than in terms of household economics and labour. What they do not recognize is that this interpretation of what love and intimacy mean is gendered. It renders domestic labour invisible, and so serves men's interests more than women's.

The fact that busy professional women are still shouldering responsibility for the domestic workload is indicative of the lack of profound change to gender roles. The dual-career couple is not as gender neutral in reality as it sounds in theory. The social construction of household work and caring as interlinked may explain why domestic work continues to be integral to a feminine gender identity. It is certainly the case that these women derive considerable emotional and personal comfort from their partners and benefit from the mutual professional respect that characterizes a successful dual-career relationship. It may well be, as Scase and Goffee argue (1993: 176), that decision-making within such partnerships is shared and reasonably egalitarian. In this way, women's increased power at work is challenging the traditional gender regime in these households. However, in practical terms, women are still the managers, planners, organizers and supervisors of domestic affairs. Retaining overall managerial responsibilities for the family appears to be one way in which women exercise power within the home and retain their gender identity.

Conclusion

In looking at the domestic basis of the managerial career, we first have to understand that being a successful senior manager currently requires an overriding commitment to work. The job consumes most waking hours and dominates life in every respect. While this is true for both women and men, it has very different implications for their personal relationships and domestic arrangements. It is producing some marked changes in patterns of household participation.

My respondents were selected for their equal status at work. However, as the study demonstrates, they are by no means equal at home. This is perhaps unsurprising. But it is interesting that as well as having to conform to the male model of working life in order to succeed, women are also adopting masculine patterns of (non)participation in the household. While male managers are still serviced by their wives, women managers are serviced by housewife substitutes in the form of other women's labour. Managing and paying for these services distinguishes women's domestic role from that of men. At the same time, they continue to undertake a disproportionate amount of housework themselves. Overall, the differences between men and women managers are much more marked in how they manage in the household than in how they manage at work.

Feminist organization theorists have largely explained the lack of women in senior management in terms of barriers within the workplace. This chapter has compared successful women and men managers and directed our attention to the significance of their position within the family. We have seen how women workers can never escape their construction as housewives. The sexual contract means that all women are defined as potential wives and mothers, while male workers are assumed to be free to perform their work. While many women sacrifice their employment opportunities in order to have children, the women in my study have mostly given up the opportunity to have children in order to pursue their careers. Most of the men in the sample are parents, and either have full-time housewives or live in one-career, rather than dual-career, households. Men do not have to make the same kind of choice between family and work.

Even so, the current conditions of work hardly afford men the chance to participate fully in family life. Indeed, the hegemonic organizational culture is inimical to family life in that it expresses itself as a 'dominant discourse of time as a commodity, symbolising productivity, commitment and personal value' (Taylor and Lewis 1993: 2). Although excellent equal opportunity policies have been designed to facilitate the combination of career and family, they have largely been focused on women, as if only women have children. These policies have not been targeted at men in a way that challenges the sexual division of domestic labour. Nor have these policies fundamentally challenged the character of the managerial career, let alone the structure of organizations. Indeed, it is a measure of the failure of equal opportunity family policies that so many of the women managers in my sample do not have children. And that those who do are heavily dependent on *other* women to do their housework and childcare. In the absence of the public provision of childcare facilities for working parents and corresponding changes in industrial culture, women have little choice but to negotiate individual solutions according to their personal priorities and resources.

Notes

1   The 'dual-career' family is distinguished from other family forms in that both partners in the household are involved in career-structured occupations and play an important role in family life. This is what distinguishes it from the 'one-career' family, in which one partner, usually the husband, has a career occupation, while the other has a 'non-career' job. These classifications are drawn against the background of the conventional middle-class marriage, comprising the male career-breadwinner and the housewife. Much more common statistically, but not of relevance to this study, is the dual-earner family, in which both partners are employed in non-career jobs.

2   Time use information comes from detailed diaries in which the respondents record all their daily activities. For an excellent analysis of recent Australian time use surveys, see Bittman and Pixley (1997: ch. 5). For a discussion of the problems of measurement of the domestic division of labour, see Warde and Hetherington (1993).

3   The notable study of managers by Scase and Goffee (1993) does include a small sample of women but they are all in junior management positions. Furthermore, their study did not collect data on housework.

4   When the effects of high status jobs on women's home lives are discussed, the focus is largely on stress. See, for example, Davidson and Cooper (1992).

Conclusion

As we move towards the twenty-first century, gender relations are a heavily contested terrain. The tremors of change reverberate throughout the lives of women and men, whose conditions of both work and personal life have undergone profound restructuring. This book is a study of men and women who work alongside each other, encompassing the experiences of both sexes in the managerial hierarchy. Recognizing that masculinity and femininity find their existence only in relation to each other, I have sought to interrogate the male gender just as closely as the female gender. Gender is present as an issue even where it seems invisible or silent in a workplace. After all, only half of the story is told if the social construction of masculinity is ignored.

I have argued that there is another dimension to this whole story. The institutions of work, not just people, must be understood as substantively gendered. The sexual division of labour is a constitutive feature of organizations, which are in turn founded on the sexual contract sealed in the home. My analysis of the gender relations of management locates them firmly in their organizational context.

The literature on women's management style, reflecting much contemporary feminist thought, has been concerned with the issue of whether women manage in the same way as men or have a distinct style of their own. I have argued that to analyse the gender power relations of the workplace in terms of arguments based on sameness and difference is not particularly illuminating. The way in which women's different style has been conceptualized has been in terms of stereotypical femininity. It is a discussion about women's values, women's culture. We are asked to celebrate an idealized femininity as demonstrated by women's greater caring, intuitive qualities. The problem is that the qualities, characteristics and culture ascribed to women originate from the historical subordination of women. Despite attempts to reclaim these values, they lie at the heart of traditional and oppressive conceptions of womanhood. In this sense arguments concerning sameness/difference can be said to incorporate essentialist discourses.

My study shows that, in practice, senior women managers manage in much the same way as senior men within the same specific context. This is because styles of management are shaped more by organizational imperatives than by the sex or personal style of specific individuals. There are important implications for gender equity strategies here. Conventional equal opportunities policies embody the 'sameness' principle by which similarly qualified women are ensured equal treatment with men. The current model of equal opportunities, managing diversity, embraces difference as its rationale for equality initiatives. It promotes the cause of women managers on the grounds that women's nurturing capacities uniquely equip them for the requirements of postmodern management. I have argued that the effect of accentuating gender differences in management is to 'naturalize' women's skills. Women's skills have been traditionally undervalued precisely because they are regarded by employers as female attributes which are natural rather than acquired through training and experience.

Engaging in a dialogue of managing diversity within the gendered workplace hierarchy is highly problematic because of the inexorable tendency for difference to be evaluated as inferiority. The revaluing of the female style and a stress on diversity rather than equality will not necessarily improve women's career prospects. It certainly deflects attention away from institutionalized sex discrimination at senior levels. Men have anyway shown themselves capable of laying claim to qualities designated as feminine where these are seen as the desirable characteristics of a manager. These new arguments about feminine values in management simply invert and thereby leave intact gender-stereotyped dichotomies. Preoccupied with fostering individual variation, diversity management forgets that all managers are constrained by the character of the organization.

While mounting a critique of the popular belief in women managers' essential difference, I have argued that systematic inequalities between men and women ensure that their experience as managers cannot be the same. The point is not that women are different, but that gender difference is the basis for the unequal distribution of power and resources. Men are still constructed as the universal standard, and it is women who are marked as 'gendered', the ones who are different, the inferior other. The problem is more complex than one of 'access'. The answer to women's exclusion is not simply to get more women to enter management. The norm for the managerial occupation remains male. Indeed, I have argued that, ironically, it is a male model of equality that women have had to adopt in order to challenge the status quo. My research confirms that to achieve positions of power, women must accommodate themselves to the organization, not the other way around. Women managers therefore pay a high price for venturing into male-dominated territory. For most women the price is too high – requiring them to sacrifice major elements of their gender identity. No equivalent sacrifice has been expected of men. Their identification with managerial power has been taken for granted, while women's absence has been cast as the problem. Even after two decades of equal opportunity policies, women are still expected to 'manage like a man'.

Although women who have made it have done so by adopting the male model, this does not mean that all men (or women) manage in precisely the same way. While in any given setting there are usually multiple masculinities present, I have argued that particular notions of manhood and masculinity are embedded in the gender regime of an institution. Managerial masculinities derive from hegemonic masculinity. But they vary in content and come to condition the actions of male and female managers alike. Men too find themselves constrained by idealized male constructs and are acutely aware of other men's constant scrutiny. Not all men endorse or aspire to the dominant male model. Some men are also alienated from the macho culture of corporate power. Indeed, most men do not succeed in becoming senior managers, and few are direct beneficiaries of the regime. The individuals of either sex who succeed are those who are prepared to be hard, those who can 'take it like a man'. Feminine and masculine qualities are not the exclusive preserve of either sex.

While women managers have been busily adapting to organizational demands, organizations themselves are currently undergoing dramatic transformations. Organizational restructuring is having a major impact not only on management jobs and careers but also on the nature of the employment relationship itself. Although the language of commitment is still commonplace, successive waves of delayering, restructuring and general downsizing have eroded the 'psychological contract' between the organization and its managers. The old paternalistic exchange relationship of undivided managerial loyalty in return for a lifetime career has been undermined.

As a result, many observers have been quick to announce the death of hierarchy and bureaucracy. There is much talk at present about the emergence of the post-bureaucratic, post-entrepreneurial, post-industrial or postmodern firm.[1] People claim this is what large corporations now look like and how they can be most accurately described. Some even assert that this is what they should look like if they don't already! I believe we should be cautious about these claims, for several reasons.

To begin with, the defining characteristics of these new forms of organization are rarely specified. Speculations about revolutionary changes abound, with little empirical substantiation. Too often the mode of analysis is to extrapolate from an atypical case study to discover a so-called general trend. Embedded in such discussions is a notion of historical inevitability in which one type of organizational form will be displaced by a newer model at the next stage of development. There is a romantic view of the past in which the organizing principle of work was the bureaucratic firm in which employees enjoyed long and secure careers. Just as this was never in reality the dominant form of organization but rather an ideal-type, so too current changes in organizations are not unfolding in a progressive or linear way. New forms of organization have by no means eclipsed older bureaucratic models. Instead, different models of organization coexist simultaneously in different sectors of the economy and in different parts of the world. Indeed, among the world's largest and most powerful organizations the predominant corporate configuration continues to be bureaucratic.[2]

The pace of change should not be exaggerated. Nevertheless, many business corporations have fundamentally reshaped their organizational structures. The companies in my study were certainly having to respond to intensified international competitive pressures and increasingly volatile markets. But despite these pressures, it is evident from my research that traditional forms of authority remain firmly in place. Consistent with this, a more aggressive, ruthless and coercive managerial style prevails. Rather than revealing any trend towards decentralized power and control, my analysis shows that a more conventional hierarchical and centralized management structure was ascendant. Furthermore, while the path and expression of an organizational career have changed, it continues to possess a remarkable resilience in the organizations I studied. Perceptions of insecurity, however, are much more marked among senior managers as a result of the turmoil brought about by the widespread 'delayering' of middle management. Similarly, the idea that there is a normal career route that can be planned for and routinely followed has lost its currency. Nonetheless, many of the features commonly attributed to the emergence of the postmodern organization can in fact be adequately accounted for in terms of fluctuations in the business cycle.

The new management literature is just as conspicuously gender-blind as its predecessor. I have argued not only that the traditional bureaucratic career was almost exclusively the province of men, but also that there is a sense in which bureaucracies were built on the exclusion of women. I have stressed that entry to senior levels was always heavily dependent upon the possession of appropriate cultural capital and related access to informal networks, processes that are themselves gendered. The post-bureaucratic firm may be said to require managers with charismatic personalities displaying qualities like flexibility, dynamism and entrepreneurialism. But this rhetoric is in tune with a rearticulation of gender, class and race biased selection criteria. If anything, their salience is increasing in a contracting managerial labour market. The riskier the business environment, the more risky it is to appoint 'others'.

In sum, corporate restructuring is causing equity issues to move down rather than up the policy agenda. Trends in management and organizational practice are moving away from facilitating equality initiatives. Shifting employment patterns, changing structures of the workplace and the rigours of highly competitive marketplaces are all taking their toll. Fairness and equity in jobs are contingent upon a kind of certainty and stability that is being rapidly disrupted in many workplaces and completely eroded in others. So-called 'bottom line' considerations of increasing profitability or efficiency mean that judgements of worth have been reconfigured around market-oriented criteria, with the demands of accountability and responsibility reaching further and further down the hierarchy. In such a context even talk of, let alone action on, equal opportunities in employment is on the wane.

Many managers and employees live in a barely concealed climate of uncertainty, if not outright fear, about the effects of more intense scrutiny of their performance. Organizations are reducing costs by employing fewer and fewer people to do more and more work, with managers putting in longer hours and achieving greater output. Partly as a result of these demands, and in response to the 'culture of commitment' stemming from modern human resource management approaches, many feel the need to demonstrate their commitment by staying late, by learning to display the requisite behaviours and by subordinating leisure, family and domestic concerns to the pressures of work.

In this context it is hard to see what managing diversity, the new 'post-equal opportunities' approach, will achieve. It fits only too well with the present drive to shift responsibility for their careers on to employees themselves. Employees are being urged to be more entrepreneurial, to think of themselves as Me, Inc. and to embrace a 'portfolio' career. To prosper in the increasingly unpredictable world of work, they must be able to reinvent themselves, to see themselves as a business. These changes are contributing to what some see as a breakdown of the social (collective) structuring of occupations and a move towards a new individualization of occupations involving the deployment of identity as a key occupational resource. This radical individualization not only – and once again – overlooks the specificity of women's relationship to work but also raises new questions about the gender politics of identity exchanges in the workplace. For instance, if the mobilization of identity as a workplace resource is universally available, we might ask whether men and women are equally placed to perform these exchanges?

The dismantling of the secure lifetime occupation combines with changes wrought by feminism to pose a severe threat to middle-class masculine identity. Men have responded and adapted in different ways to working alongside, and competing with, women. Most modern corporation men accept equal opportunities for professional women, and as a result there is much less overt sex discrimination. Inevitably, however, there are strong feelings of resentment against women who are gaining a foothold in senior management at a time when career ladders are shrinking for both sexes. Some men, by their actions or inaction, are obstructing changes that will inevitably undermine their own hegemony. It is no coincidence that we are witnessing the appearance of a new discourse of men's disadvantage in which men are constructed as those who suffer discrimination to provide equal opportunities for women. There is also a perception that new work practices may feminize men by requiring them to be more flexible or adaptive, to switch between different modes and types of work, and to engage in different tasks in parallel or simultaneously. In this sense men may well feel that, rather than women levelling up to them, they are levelling down to women.

When the spotlight is turned on equality between women and men at senior levels, we find signs of increasing divisions between women.

New forms of stratification appear to be emerging in which a minority of women work alongside men on comparable terms and conditions of employment. Most women, however, become marginalized from the core labour market in part-time, casualized work. Women managers are largely assimilated to a male model of full-time work by virtue of their 'freedom' to exchange their labour with employers on similar terms to men. While still accountable for family welfare, to the extent that they can purchase family and domestic services these women are relieved of the fetters to which most of their sex remain subject. Few women at the top have children, and the ones who do also have nannies. The ability of women managers to track their male counterparts is dependent on the existence of female domestic help and so generates further inequalities between women.

For many feminists the recognition that successful women now build their careers either on childlessness or by relying on other women's cheap domestic labour highlights a cruel dilemma. It lays bare the material differences between women, particularly those based on class and race. Yet the contracting out of domestic service is not new and continues to exist in most of the world. We tend to forget that the historical period during which middle-class housewives in countries such as the US and UK had to do their own domestic labour was something of an aberration. The decline of paid and unpaid servants (including family members such as unmarried daughters and maiden aunts) as household workers from the interwar period onwards placed most women on the same footing in relation to their performance of domestic labour. They were equally exposed to constructions of femininity centred on the ideology of the housewife and the symbolic importance of the home. With the resurgence of paid domestic services, middle-class women are again managing other women's labour within their homes. Employer–employee relations between women have been re-established. This has no doubt contributed to a heightened awareness of women's different identities based on increasingly dissimilar life experiences.

Resonating with the culture of individualization in the workplace, women are seeking individual solutions to the social reproduction of the household. They are not responding to the demands of full-time employment by renegotiating the sexual contract of marriage. Indeed, that option is one women are backing away from, by contracting out their domestic work rather than confronting male power in the home. Men's refusal to play an equal part in all forms of domestic labour is one of the key mechanisms through which gender inequalities are reproduced. Yet many middle-class women are reluctant to acknowledge the way in which waged domestic labour works to the ultimate benefit of men. Until men demand the opportunity for full participation in the home, women will continue to pay the price for equal opportunities at work.

If women have difficulty confronting male power in the home, there are also problems with women's relationship to power in the workplace. While there has been a growing interest in multiple masculinities in organizational studies, much less attention has been paid to the existence of multiple femininities at work. By focusing in this study on a group of women pioneering in male territory, I have stressed the traps they encounter as they come up against conventional notions of femaleness. The sexualization of the employment relationship situates women managers in a contradictory relationship to power – they must be both businesslike and attractive. The legitimacy of their authority is always open to question.

An issue from which feminists tend to shy away is that many women also undermine other women's authority. Various constructions of femininity which women deploy in relating to men in power involve being flirtatious, admiring and generally supportive. In this way, women are actively reconstituting hetereosexualized forms of dominance and subordination. They therefore can have trouble dealing with women in positions of power, because the strategies that they are accustomed to using with men are inappropriate for female bosses. Because women have internalized gender hierarchies, it seems almost proper for a male to be in a superior position. In the case of men, power is eroticized. This complex intertwining of power with sexuality means that powerful women provoke anxieties and ambivalence in women as well as men.

The fact that women carry less authority may shape their attitudes towards the exercise of power. The belief that women are naturally more consensual, more inclined to negotiate, is hard to dislodge. Arguably, it is precisely because the seeking and holding of power is inimical to the construction of femininity that women may have to be more consultative. This style of management could be the expression of a relative lack of power rather than a characteristic of womanhood *per se*. In society at large, women are identified with emotional and relational work. But to get to the top women have largely had to abandon this role. Just as they have to delegate domestic work to paid helpers, so too they have to relegate emotional labour in the workplace, thereby relinquishing core aspects of prescribed femininity in both the public and private spheres.

More women than ever before are in positions of power. Their presence is disruptive of established gender relations at work. Feminism and sex equality policies, while not transformative in themselves, have contributed to changing corporate sensibilities. They have given women a language for interpreting organizational processes that sustain discrimination, as well as a glimpse of a different future. They have also lifted the roof off women's aspirations. Many women now share men's expectations of a continuous career, and are willing to be competitive with men.

In this book I argue that far from patenting a new feminine management style, women must generally 'manage like a man' to succeed. This is not to say, however, that women are or can simply emulate men. Rather, managerial women are forging what might be thought of as new hybrid forms of gender identity, in which their subjectivity centres as much on the workplace as it does for men. Even their participation in domestic labour takes on the character of management. Investing more of their purchasing power and less of their gender identity in domesticity, these women are challenging the gender regimes of both the workplace and the home. For women and men, opportunities for realizing alternative visions are overshadowed by the continued primacy of paid work as the source of status and meaning in contemporary culture.

Notes

1   See for example, Casey (1995), Clegg (1990), Heckscher (1995), Kanter (1992).
2   See Goffee and Scase (1995). Edwards et al. (1996: 61) concur, concluding an article based on their survey of multinational companies thus: 'New forms of organisation are not only rare but also share important features, notably the meeting of targets and the pursuit of the corporate vision, with older bureaucracies.'

Bibliography

Acker, J. (1990) Hierarchies, jobs, bodies: a theory of gendered organizations. *Gender and Society*, 4, 139–58.

Adkins, L. (1995) *Gendered Work: Sexuality, Family and the Labour Market*. Buckingham: Open University Press.

Adler, N. and Izraeli, D. (1994) *Competitive Frontiers: Women Managers in a Global Economy*. Oxford: Blackwell.

Arber, S. and Ginn, J. (1995) The mirage of gender equality: occupational success in the labour market and within marriage. *British Journal of Sociology*, 46/1, 21–43.

Arnold, V. and Davidson, M. (1990) Adopt a mentor – the new way ahead for women managers? *Women in Management Review and Abstracts*, 5/1, 10–19.

Ashburner, L. (1994) Women in management careers: opportunities and outcomes. In J. Evetts (ed.), *Women and Career*, London: Longman.

Australian Government (1995) *Enterprising Nation*, Report on Leadership and Management Skills. Canberra: Australian Government Publishing Service.

Bacchi, C. (1990) *Same Difference: Feminism and Sexual Difference*. Sydney: Allen and Unwin.

Bacchi, C. (1996) *The Politics of Affirmative Action*. London: Sage.

Bacharach, S. and Lawler, E. (1980) *Power and Politics in Organizations*. San Francisco: Jossey-Bass.

Backett, K. (1987) The negotiation of fatherhood. In C. Lewis and M. O'Brien (eds), *Reassessing Fatherhood: New Observations on Fathers and the Modern Family*, London: Sage.

Barrett, M. (1980) *Women's Oppression Today*. London: Verso.

Barrett, M. and Phillips, A. (eds) (1992) *Destabilizing Theory*. Cambridge: Polity Press.

Beck, U. and Beck-Gernsheim, E. (1995)   *The Normal Chaos of Love.*
Cambridge: Polity Press.
Becker, G. (1985)   Human capital, effort, and the sexual division of labor.
Journal of Labor Economics, 3/2, 33–58.
Beechey, V. (1978)   Women and production: a critical analysis of some
sociological theories of women's work. In A. Kuhn and A. Wolpe (eds),
Feminism and Materialism, London: Routledge.
Beechey, V. (1987)   *Unequal Work.* London: Verso.
Bendix, R. (1966)   *Work and Authority in Industry.* New York: John Wiley.
Benokraitis, N. and Feagin, J. (1995)   *Modern Sexism: Blatant, Subtle and
Covert Discrimination*, 2nd edn. Englewood Cliffs, N.J.: Prentice Hall.
Bittman, M. and Lovejoy, F. (1993)   Domestic power: negotiating an
unequal division of labour within a framework of equality. *Australian
and New Zealand Journal of Sociology*, 29, 302–21.
Bittman, M. and Pixley, J. (1997)   *The Double Life of the Family: Myth,
Hope and Experience.* St Leonards: Allen and Unwin.
Blyton, P. and Turnbull, P. (eds) (1992)   *Reassessing Human Resource
Management.* London: Sage.
Brannen, J. and Moss, P. (1991)   *Managing Mothers: Dual Earner
Households after Maternity Leave.* London: Unwin Hyman.
Brannen, J., Mészáros, G., Moss, P. and Poland, G. (1994)   Employment
and family life: a review of research in the UK (1980–1994). Department
of Employment, Research Series, no. 41.
Braverman, H. (1974)   *Labor and Monopoly Capital: The Degradation of
Work in the Twentieth Century.* New York: Monthly Review Press.
Brenner, O. C., Tomkiewicz, J. and Schein, V. E. (1989)   The relationship
between sex role stereotypes and requisite management characteristics.
Academy of Management Journal, 32, 662–9.
British Institute of Management (1994)   *Management Development to the
Millennium.* London: BIM.
British NHS Women's Unit (1994)   Top managers. Creative Career Paths
in the National Health Service, report no. 1.
Brown, P. and Scase, R. (1994)   *Higher Education and Corporate Realities.*
London: UCL Press.
Burrell, G. (1984)   Sex and organizational analysis. *Organization Studies*,
5/2, 97–118.
Burton, C. (1991)   *The Promise and the Price: The Struggle for Equal
Opportunity in Women's Employment.* Sydney: Allen and Unwin.
Business in the Community (1996)   *Opportunity 2000: Fifth Year Review.*
London: Business in the Community.
Butler, J. (1990)   *Gender Trouble.* New York: Routledge.
Calas, M. and Smircich, L. (1992)   Using the 'F' word: feminist theories
and the social consequences of organizational research. In A. Mills and
P. Tancred (eds), *Gendering Organizational Analysis*, London: Sage.
Casey, C. (1995)   *Work, Self and Society.* London: Routledge.
Charlesworth, K. (1997)   A question of balance? A survey of managers'

changing professional and personal roles. British Institute of Management Report, London.

Chodorow, N. (1978) *The Reproduction of Mothering.* Berkeley: University of California Press.

Clegg, S. (1989) *Frameworks of Power.* London: Sage.

Clegg, S. (1990) *Modern Organisations.* London: Sage.

Cockburn, C. (1983) *Brothers: Male Dominance and Technological Change.* London: Pluto Press.

Cockburn, C. (1985) *Machinery of Dominance.* London: Pluto Press.

Cockburn, C. (1989) Equal opportunities: the short and long agenda. *Industrial Relations Journal,* 20/3, 213–25.

Cockburn, C. (1991) *In the Way of Women: Men's Resistance to Sex Equality in Organizations.* London: Macmillan.

Coe, T. (1992) The key to the men's club. British Institute of Management Report, London.

Cohn, S. (1985) *The Process of Occupational Sex Typing: The Feminisation of Clerical Labour in Great Britain.* Philadelphia: Temple University Press.

Collier, R. (1995) *Combating Sexual Harassment in the Workplace.* Buckingham: Open University Press.

Collins, R. (1979) *The Credential Society.* Orlando: Academic Press.

Collinson, D. and Collinson, M. (1989) Sexuality in the workplace: the domination of men's sexuality. In J. Hearn et al. (eds), *The Sexuality of Organization,* London: Sage.

Collinson, D. and Hearn, J. (1994) Naming men as men: implications for work organization and management. *Gender, Work and Organization,* 1/1, 2–22.

Collinson, D., Knights, D. and Collinson, M. (1990) *Managing to Discriminate.* London: Routledge.

Collinson, M. and Collinson, D. (1996) It's only Dick: the sexual harassment of women managers in insurance sales. *Work, Employment and Society,* 10, 29–56.

Connell, R. (1987) *Gender and Power.* Cambridge: Polity Press.

Connell, R. (1995) *Masculinities.* Cambridge: Polity Press.

Copeland, L. (1988a) Valuing diversity, part 1: Making the most of cultural difference at the workplace. *Personnel,* June, 53–60.

Copeland, L. (1988b) Valuing diversity, part 2: Pioneers and champions of change. *Personnel,* July, 44–9.

Corrigan, P. and Sayer, D. (1985) *The Great Arch.* Oxford: Blackwell.

Coward, R. (1993) *Our Treacherous Hearts: Why Women Let Men Get their Way.* London: Faber and Faber.

Cox, E. and Leonard, H. (1991) From Ummm . . . to Aha!: recognising women's skills. Women's Research and Employment Initiatives Program, Canberra: Australian Government Publishing Service.

Coyle, A. (1989) Women in management: a suitable case for treatment? *Feminist Review,* 31, Spring, 117–25.

Crompton, R. (1986)   Women and the 'service class'. In R. Crompton and M. Mann (eds), *Gender and Stratification*, Cambridge: Polity Press.

Crompton, R. and Sanderson, K. (1990)   *Gendered Jobs and Social Change.* London: Unwin Hyman.

Curran, M. (1988)   Gender and recruitment: people and places in the labour market. *Work, Employment and Society*, 2/3, 335–51.

Davidson, M. and Cooper, G. (1992)   *Shattering the Glass Ceiling: The Woman Manager.* London: Paul Chapman.

Dex, S. (1987)   *Women's Occupational Mobility: A Lifetime Perspective.* London: Macmillan.

Dickens, L. (1994)   Wasted resources? Equal opportunities in employment. In K. Sisson (ed.), *Personnel Management*, Oxford: Blackwell.

DiTomaso, N. (1989)   Sexuality in the workplace: discrimination and harassment. In J. Hearn et al. (eds), *The Sexuality of Organization*, London: Sage.

Dubin, R. (1956)   Industrial workers' worlds: a study of the 'central life interests' of industrial workers. *Social Problems*, 3, 131–42.

Duncombe, J. and Marsden, D. (1995)   'Workaholics' and 'whingeing women': theorising intimacy and emotion work: the last frontier of gender inequality? *Sociological Review*, 43/1, 150–69.

Eagly, A. and Johnson, B. (1990)   Gender and leadership style: a meta-analysis. *Psychological Bulletin*, 108/2, 233–56.

Edwards, P. K., Armstrong, P., Marginson, P. and Purcell, J. (1996) Towards the transnational company? The global structure and organisation of multinational firms. In R. Crompton, D. Gallie and K. Purcell (eds), *Changing Forms of Employment*, London: Routledge.

Eichenbaum, L. and Orbach, S. (1982)   *Outside In . . . Inside Out.* Harmondsworth: Penguin.

Eisenstein, H. (1984)   *Contemporary Feminist Thought.* London: Allen and Unwin.

England, P. (1982)   The failure of human capital theory to explain occupational sex segregation. *Journal of Human Resources*, 17/3, 358–70.

Epstein, C. Fuchs (1988)   *Deceptive Distinctions: Sex, Gender, and the Social Order.* New Haven: Yale University Press.

Evetts, J. (1996)   *Gender and Career in Science and Engineering.* London: Taylor and Francis.

Fagenson, E. (1986)   Women's work orientation: something old, something new. *Group and Organization Studies*, 11/1, 75–100.

Fagenson, E. (1990)   At the heart of women in management research: theoretical and methodological approaches and their biases. *Journal of Business Ethics*, 9, 267–74.

Fagenson, E. (ed.) (1993)   *Women in Management: Trends, Issues, and Challenges in Managerial Diversity.* Newbury Park: Sage.

Feldberg, R. and Glenn, E. (1984)   Male and female: job versus gender models in the sociology of work. In J. Siltanen and M. Stanworth (eds), *Women in the Public Sphere*, London: Hutchinson.

Ferguson, K. (1984) *The Feminist Case against Bureaucracy.* Philadelphia: Temple University Press.

Ferrario, M. (1994) Women as managerial leaders. In M. Davidson and R. Burke (eds), *Women in Management,* London: Paul Chapman.

Fierman, J. (1990) Do women manage differently? *Fortune,* 17 Dec., 71–4.

Finch, J. (1983) *Married to the Job: Wives' Incorporation in Men's Work.* London: Allen and Unwin.

Fromm, E. (1949) *Man for Himself: An Enquiry into the Psychology of Ethics.* London: Routledge and Kegan Paul.

Gershuny, J. and Robinson, J. (1988) Historical changes in the household division of labour. *Demography,* 25/4, 537–52.

Gershuny, J., Godwin, M. and Jones, S. (1994) The domestic labour revolution: a process of lagged adaption. In M. Anderson et al. (eds), *The Social and Political Economy of the Household,* Oxford: Oxford University Press.

Gherardi, S. (1995) *Gender, Symbolism and Organizational Cultures.* London: Sage.

Giddens, A. (1992) *The Transformation of Intimacy.* Cambridge: Polity Press.

Gilligan, C. (1982) *In a Different Voice: Psychological Theory and Women's Development.* Cambridge: Harvard University Press.

Goffee, R. and Scase, R. (1992) Organizational change and the corporate career: the restructuring of managers' job aspirations. *Human Relations,* 45/4, 363–84.

Goffee, R. and Scase, R. (1995) *Corporate Realities.* London: Routledge.

Goffman, E. (1967) *Interaction Ritual: Essays on Face-to-Face Behavior.* New York: Anchor Books.

Goffman, E. (1969) *The Presentation of Self in Everyday Life.* Harmondsworth: Penguin.

Goldthorpe, J. et al. (1969) *The Affluent Worker in the Class Structure.* Cambridge: Cambridge University Press.

Gordon, G., DiTomaso, N. and Farris, G. F. (1991) Managing diversity in R&D groups. *Research Technology Management,* 34/1, 18–23.

Grant, J. and Porter, P. (1994) Women managers: the construction of gender in the workplace. *Australian and New Zealand Journal of Sociology,* 30/2, 149–61.

Green, E. and Cassell, C. (1996) Women managers, gendered cultural processes and organisational change. *Gender, Work and Organization,* 3/3, 168–78.

Greenslade, M. (1991) Managing diversity: lessons from the United States. *Personnel Management,* Dec., 28–33.

Gregg, P. and Machin, S. (1993) Is the glass ceiling cracking? Gender compensation differentials and access to promotion among UK executives. National Institute of Economic and Social Research, Discussion Paper 50.

Gregson, N. and Lowe, M. (1993) Renegotiating the domestic division of labour? A study of dual career households in north east and south east England. *Sociological Review*, 41/3, 475–505.

Gregson, N. and Lowe, M. (1994)   *Servicing the Middle Classes*. London: Routledge.

Guest, D. (1992)   Employee commitment and control. In J. Hartley and G. Stephenson (eds), *Employment Relations*, Oxford: Blackwell.

Hacker, S. (1981)   The culture of engineering: woman, workplace and machine. *Women's Studies International Quarterly*, 4, 341–53.

Hadjifotiou, N. (1983)   *Women and Harassment at Work*. London: Pluto Press.

Hakim, C. (1993)   The myth of rising female employment. *Work, Employment and Society*, 7/1, 97–120.

Hakim, C. (1995)   Five feminist myths about women's employment. *British Journal of Sociology*, 46/3, 429–55.

Halford, S. (1992)   Feminist change in a patriarchal organisation. In M. Savage and A. Witz (eds), *Gender and Bureaucracy*, Oxford: Blackwell.

Handy, C. (1994)   *The Empty Raincoat*. London: Hutchinson.

Harding, S. (1986)   *The Science Question in Feminism*. Ithaca: Cornell University Press.

Hearn, J. and Parkin, W. (1987)   *Sex at Work: The Power and Paradox of Organization Sexuality*. Brighton: Wheatsheaf Books.

Hearn, J., Sheppard, D., Tancred-Sheriff, P. and Burrell, G. (eds) (1989)   *The Sexuality of Organization*. London: Sage.

Heckscher, C. (1995)   *White Collar Blues: Management Loyalties in an Age of Corporate Restructuring*. New York: Basic Books.

Heilman, M., Block, C., Mantell, R. and Simon, M. (1989)   Has anything changed? Current characterizations of men, women, and managers. *Journal of Applied Psychology*, 74/6, 935–42.

Hennig, M. and Jardim, A. (1979)   *The Managerial Woman*. London: Pan Books.

Hirsch, M. and Keller, E. (eds) (1990)   *Conflicts in Feminism*. New York: Routledge.

Hochschild, A. (1983)   *The Managed Heart: Commercialization of Human Feeling*. Berkeley: University of California Press.

Hochschild, A. (1990)   *The Second Shift: Working Parents and the Revolution at Home*. London: Piatkus.

Industrial Relations Services (1992)   Sexual harassment at the workplace. Employment Review no. 513, 6–15.

Jackall, R. (1988)   *Moral Mazes: The World of Corporate Managers*. New York: Oxford University Press.

Jacobs, J. (1992)   Women's entry into management: trends in earnings, authority and values among salaried managers. *Administrative Science Quarterly*, 37, 282–301.

Jaggar, A. (1989)   Love and knowledge: emotion in feminist epistemology. In A. Jaggar and S. Bordo (eds), *Gender/Body/Knowledge: Feminist*

Reconstructions of Being and Knowing, New Brunswick: Rutgers University Press.

James, N. (1989) Emotional labour: skill and work in the social regulation of feelings. *Sociological Review*, 37/1, 15–42.

Jenkins, R. (1986) *Racism and Recruitment*. Cambridge: Cambridge University Press.

Jewson, N. and Mason, D. (1986) The theory and practice of equal opportunities policies: liberal and radical approaches. *Sociological Review*, 34/2, 307–34.

Kanter, R. M. (1977) *Men and Women of the Corporation*. New York: Basic Books.

Kanter, R. M. (1983) *The Change Masters: Innovations for Productivity in the American Corporation*. New York: Simon and Schuster.

Kanter, R. M. (1989) *When Giants Learn to Dance: Mastering the Challenge of Strategy, Management, and Careers in the 1990s*. New York: Simon and Schuster.

Kanter, R. M. (1992) *The Challenge of Organisational Change*. New York: Free Press.

Kessler, I. (1994) Performance pay. In K. Sisson (ed.), *Personnel Management*, Oxford: Blackwell.

Kiernan, K. (1992) Men and women at work and at home. In R. Jowell et al. (eds), *British Social Attitudes, 9th Report*, Cambridge: Dartmouth.

Korenman, S. and Neumark, D. (1992) Marriage, motherhood and wages. *Journal of Human Resources*, 27/2, 233–55.

Kwolek-Folland, A. (1994) *Engendering Business: Men and Women in the Corporate Office, 1870–1930*. Baltimore: Johns Hopkins University Press.

Legge, K. (1987) Women in personnel management. In A. Spencer and D. Podmore (eds), *In a Man's World*, London: Tavistock.

Legge, K. (1994) Managing cultures: fact or fiction? In K. Sisson (ed.), *Personnel Management*, Oxford: Blackwell.

Lewis, S. (1997) 'Family friendly' employment policies: a route to changing organizational culture or playing about at the margins? *Gender, Work and Organization*, 4/1, 13–23.

Liff, S. (1996) Managing diversity: new opportunities for women? Warwick Papers in Industrial Relations, no. 57.

Liff, S. and Wajcman, J. (1996) 'Sameness' and 'difference' revisited: which way forward for equal opportunity initiatives? *Journal of Management Studies*, 33/1, 79–94.

Lloyd, G. (1984) *The Man of Reason*. London: Methuen.

Loden, M. (1985) *Feminine Leadership, or How to Succeed in Business without being One of the Boys*. New York: Times Books.

Marginson, P., Armstrong, P., Edwards, P. K. and Purcell, J. (1993) The control of industrial relations in large companies: an initial analysis of the second company level industrial relations survey. Warwick Papers in Industrial Relations, no. 45.

Marshall, J. (1984) *Women Managers: Travellers in a Male World.* Chichester: John Wiley.

Marshall, J. (1995) *Women Managers Moving On.* London: Routledge.

Martin, P. (1993) Feminist practice in organizations. In E. Fagenson (ed.), *Women in Management*, Newbury Park: Sage.

Mead, G. (1934) *Mind, Self and Society.* Chicago: University of Chicago Press.

Mills, A. and Tancred, P. (1992) *Gendering Organizational Analysis.* London: Sage.

Morris, L. (1990) *The Workings of the Household.* Cambridge: Polity Press.

Mumby, D. and Putnam, L. (1992) The politics of emotion: a feminist reading of bounded rationality. *Academy of Management Review*, 17/3, 465–86.

Myrdal, A. and Klein, V. (1956) *Women's Two Roles.* London: Routledge.

Newell, H. and Dopson, S. (1996) Muddle in the middle: organizational restructuring and middle management careers. *Personnel Review*, 25/4, 4–20.

Nicholson, L. (ed.) (1990) *Feminism/Postmodernism.* London: Routledge.

Nicholson, N. and West, M. (eds) (1988) *Managerial Job Change: Men and Women in Transition.* Cambridge: Cambridge University Press.

Olson, C. and Becker, B. (1983) Sex discrimination in the promotion process. *Industrial and Labor Relations Review*, 36, 624–41.

Pahl, J. and Pahl, R. (1971) *Managers and their Wives.* Harmondsworth: Penguin.

Pahl, R. (1995) *After Success.* Cambridge: Polity Press.

Palmer, C. and Moon, G. (1997) *Discrimination at Work.* London: Legal Action Group.

Parsons. T. and Bales, R. (1956) *Family Socialization and Interaction Patterns.* London: Routledge.

Pateman, C. (1988) *The Sexual Contract.* Cambridge: Polity Press.

Pateman, C. (1989) *The Disorder of Women.* Cambridge: Polity Press.

Peters, T. and Waterman, R. (1982) *In Search of Excellence.* New York: Harper and Row.

Phillips, A. and Taylor, B. (1980) Sex and skill: notes towards a feminist economics. *Feminist Review*, 6, 79–88.

Powell, G. (1993) *Women and Men in Management.* Newbury Park: Sage.

Price, R. and Bain, G. (1976) Union growth revisited. *British Journal of Industrial Relations*, 14/3, 339–55.

Pringle, R. (1988) *Secretaries Talk.* Sydney: Allen and Unwin.

Purcell, K. (1988) Gender and the experience of employment. In D. Gallie, *Employment in Britain*, Oxford: Blackwell.

Radin, M. (1991) Affirmative action rhetoric. *Social Philosophy and Policy*, 8/2, 130–49.

Rapoport, R. and Rapoport, R. (1971) *Dual-Career Families.* Harmondsworth: Penguin.

Reskin, B. and Roos, P. (1990) *Job Queues, Gender Queues: Explaining*

Women's Inroads into Male Occupations. Philadelphia: Temple University Press.

Reskin, B. and Ross, C. (1992) Jobs, authority and earnings among managers: the continuing significance of sex. *Work and Occupations*, 19/4, 342–65.

Riley, D. (1988) *'Am I That Name?' Feminism and the Category of 'Women' in History*. Basingstoke: Macmillan.

Roper, M. (1994) *Masculinity and the British Organization Man since 1945*. Oxford: Oxford University Press.

Rosener, J. (1990) Ways women lead. *Harvard Business Review*, Dec., 199–225.

Rousseau, D. M. (1995) *Psychological Contracts in Organizations: Understanding Written and Unwritten Agreements*. Thousand Oaks, Calif.: Sage.

Rubery, J. (1992) Pay, gender and the social dimension to Europe. *British Journal of Industrial Relations*, 30/4, 605–22.

Rubery, J. (1995) The low-paid and the unorganised. In P. Edwards (ed.), *Industrial Relations: Theory and Practice in Britain*, Oxford: Blackwell.

Rubin, J. (1997) Gender, equality and the culture of organizational assessment. *Gender, Work and Organization*, 4, 24–34.

Runciman, W. (1966) *Relative Deprivation and Social Justice*. London: Routledge and Kegan Paul.

Savage, M. (1992) Women's expertise, men's authority: gendered organization and the contemporary middle class. In M. Savage and A. Witz (eds), *Gender and Bureaucracy*, Oxford: Blackwell.

Savage, M. and Witz, A. (1992) *Gender and Bureaucracy*. Oxford: Blackwell.

Scase, R. and Goffee, R. (1993) *Reluctant Managers*. London: Routledge.

Schein, V. (1973) The relationship between sex role stereotypes and requisite management characteristics. *Journal of Applied Psychology*, 57, 95–100.

Schein, V. (1994) Managerial sex typing: a persistent and pervasive barrier to women's opportunities. In M. Davidson and R. Burke (eds), *Women in Management: Current Research Issues*, London: Paul Chapman.

Schor, N. (1994) Introduction. In N. Schor and E. Weed (eds), *The Essential Difference*, Bloomington: Indiana University Press.

Schwartz, F. (1992) *Breaking with Tradition: Women and Work, the New Facts of Life*. New York: Time Warner.

Scott, J. (1988) *Gender and the Politics of History*. New York: Columbia University Press.

Shaw, J. and Perrons, D. (eds) (1995) *Making Gender Work: Managing Equal Opportunities*. Buckingham: Open University Press.

Sheppard, D. (1989) Organizations, power and sexuality: the image and self-image of women managers. In J. Hearn et al. (eds), *The Sexuality of Organization*, London: Sage.

Sisson, K. (1994a) Personnel management: paradigms, practice and prospects. In K. Sisson (ed.), *Personnel Management*, Oxford: Blackwell.

Sisson, K. (ed.) (1994b)   *Personnel Management*. Oxford: Blackwell.

Sloan, P. (1990)   Sex differentials: structure, stability and change. In M. Gregory and A. Thomson (eds), *A Portrait of Pay, 1970–1982*, Oxford: Clarendon Press.

Smircich, L. (1983)   Concepts of culture and organisational analysis. *Administrative Science Quarterly*, 28/3, 339–58.

Smith, D. (1987)   *The Everyday World as Problematic*. Milton Keynes: Open University Press.

Smith, V. (1990)   *Managing in the Corporate Interest*. Berkeley: University of California Press.

Stanko, E. (1988)   Keeping women in and out of line: sexual harassment and occupational segregation. In S. Walby (ed.), *Gender Segregation*, Milton Keynes: Open University Press.

Stewart, R. (1967)   *Managers and their Jobs*. London: Macmillan.

Storey, J. (1992)   *Developments in the Management of Human Resources*. Oxford: Blackwell.

Storey, J., Edwards, P. and Sisson, K. (1997)   *Managers in the Making: Careers, Development and Control in Corporate Britain and Japan*. London: Sage.

Storey, J. et al. (1992)   Managerial careers and management development: a comparative analysis of Britain and Japan. *Human Resource Management Journal*, 1/3, 33–57.

Tannen, D. (1993)   *You Just Don't Understand: Women and Men in Conversation*. London: Virago.

Tanton, M. (ed.) (1994)   *Women in Management*. London: Routledge.

Taylor, K. and Lewis, S. (1993)   Family friendly employment policies in the accountancy profession. Paper presented at the Northern Branch conference on Women in Management, Sept.

Thomas, R. (1990)   From affirmative action to affirming diversity. *Harvard Business Review*, 68/1–3, 107–17.

Thompson, L. (1991)   Family work: women's sense of fairness. *Journal of Family Issues*, 12/2, 181–96.

Van Maanen, J. and Kunda, G. (1989)   Real feelings: emotional expression and organizational culture. *Research in Organizational Behavior*, 11, 43–103.

Wajcman, J. (1981)   Work and the family: who gets the best of both worlds? In Cambridge Women's Studies Group (ed.), *Women in Society: Interdisciplinary Essays*, London: Virago.

Wajcman, J. (1991)   *Feminism Confronts Technology*. Cambridge: Polity Press; University Park: Penn State Press.

Wajcman, J. (ed.) (1993)   Organisations, gender and power. Warwick Papers in Industrial Relations, no. 48.

Wajcman, J. (1996)   Women and men managers: careers and equal opportunities. In R. Crompton, D. Gallie and K. Purcell (eds), *Changing Forms of Employment*, London: Routledge.

Walby, S. (1986) *Patriarchy at Work.* Cambridge: Polity Press.
Walby, S. (ed.) (1988) *Gender Segregation at Work.* Milton Keynes: Open University Press.
Waldfogel, J. (1997) The effect of children on women's wages. *American Sociological Review*, 62, 209–17.
Warde, A. and Hetherington, K. (1993) A changing domestic division of labour? Issues of measurement and interpretation. *Work, Employment and Society*, 7/1, 23–45.
Webb, J. and Liff, S. (1988) Play the white man: the social construction of fairness and competition in equal opportunities policies. *Sociological Review*, 36/3, 532–51.
Wheelock, J. (1990) *Husbands at Home: The Domestic Economy in a Post Industrial Society.* London: Routledge.
Whyte, W. (1957) *The Organization Man.* London: Cape.
Willis, P. (1977) *Learning to Labour: How Working Class Kids Get Working Class Jobs.* London: Saxon House.
Witz, A. (1992) *Patriarchy and Professions.* London: Routledge.
Witz, A. (1993) Gender and bureaucracy: feminist concerns. In J. Wajcman (ed.), 'Organisations, gender and power', Warwick Papers in Industrial Relations, no. 48.
Wood, S. (1989) New wave management? Review article. *Work, Employment and Society*, 3/3, 379–402.
Wright, E. O. and Baxter, J. (1995) The gender gap in workplace authority: a cross-national study. *American Sociological Review*, 60, 407–35.
Young, I. (1990) *Justice and the Politics of Difference.* Princeton: Princeton University Press.
Young, I. (1994) Gender as seriality: thinking about women as a social collective. *Signs*, 19/3, 713–38.
Young, M. and Willmott, P. (1975) *The Symmetrical Family.* Harmondsworth: Penguin.
Zimmeck, M. (1992) Marry in haste, repent at leisure: women, bureaucracy and the Post Office, 1870–1920. In M. Savage and A. Witz (eds), *Gender and Bureaucracy*, Oxford: Blackwell.

Index